BETWEEN MOUNTAIN AND SEA

Norman MacCaig (1910–96) was born and educated
in Edinburgh. He attended the Royal High School,
studied Classics at the University and went on to train
as a schoolteacher. When he retired from teaching he
was appointed as Creative Writer in Residence at the
University of Edinburgh and then joined the staff at
the University of Stirling. He loved Edinburgh and lived
there all his life but found a special source of creative
enrichment for himself and his family by making lengthy
visits to Assynt every summer.

MacCaig was awarded the Queen's Gold Medal for
Poetry and many other distinctions but is best
remembered for his teaching and reading, his fruitful
influence on younger writers, and most of all for the
poems that celebrated the living world so memorably
over so many years.

BETWEEN MOUNTAIN AND SEA

POEMS FROM ASSYNT

NORMAN MacCAIG

Edited and introduced by
RODERICK WATSON

Foreword by
EWEN McCAIG

First published in paperback in Great Britain in 2018 by
Polygon, an imprint of Birlinn Ltd

West Newington House
10 Newington Road
Edinburgh EH9 1QS

www.polygonbooks.co.uk

ISBN 978 1 84697 449 6
eBook ISBN 978 1 78885 029 2

British Library Cataloguing-in-Publication Data
A catalogue record for this book is available on
request from the British Library.

Typeset by Polygon, Edinburgh
Printed and bound in Great Britain by Clays Ltd, Elcograf S.p.A.

CONTENTS

'LONG JOURNEY BACK'

'ENVIABLE LANDSCAPES'

'THE MISTY LANDSCAPE OF HISTORY'

'BACK AGAIN'

'HONEY AND SALT'

FOREWORD

There are about 800 poems in the published work of
Norman MacCaig, of which some 140 focus mainly
on the Assynt landscape or people. Their significance
appears to outweigh the numeric proportion, partly
because of when they were written (most were from the
1960s onwards when, in my view, his best work was
produced) but mainly because of their direct expression
and the intense personal commitment to the landscape
and people. The poems in this collection span a period of
more than forty years. Reading through them, it becomes
clear that his emotional ties to the area remained
constant throughout his life. The late poems, written
when he could no longer visit Assynt, became tinged with
nostalgia, but their subjects are no less vividly depicted.

Although the poems certainly stand alone for any
reader, they carry a personal significance for me because
they are about shared experiences. Although this can also
be said about numerous poems amongst his other work
(which I would never wish to see overshadowed by the
Assynt poems), I can see that the directness of experience
that my father believed was needed to create a good poem
is most consistently present in the Assynt poetry. Despite
long familiarity with my father's work, preparation
of this book was the first occasion on which I read the
Assynt poems as a discrete group. I was surprised by the
intensification of the poetic experience and the depth
of meaning projected by this work as a whole, which

certainly seems more than the sum of its parts. That, for me, amply justifies this volume, which illustrates one man's sustained and deeply felt engagement with a special place and the people that he found there.

The McCaigs first went to Assynt in 1947, and a lengthy sequence of summer visits followed. Getting to know the place and the people intimately took time. The landscapes were not explored by my father as a romantic Wordsworthian rambler. He was an enthusiastic and bloodthirsty fisherman and, although he loved walking through the Assynt landscape, it was the fishing that got him out of his chair. His growing knowledge of the land can be linked to the widening exploration of the fishing possibilities that we undertook when I was young. Communication with a range of local people also took some years to build up, partly because we (and others) did not have a car in the early times and the community was widespread. There is little doubt that, for him, the landscape and the community were aspects of a singular thing and the development of his many local friendships was as important and (in the poetic sense) meaningful as the landscape.

The first years of Assynt holidays were spent in Achmelvich with a move to Inverkirkaig in the mid-1970s. A point I noted during the preparation of this book was the large number of poems relating to the early years in Achmelvich, some appearing decades later. Many of the Achmelvich poems are only recognisable as Assynt poems because of my personal memories: for example, 'Water tap', where the surroundings confirm it is the tap by the road behind our (unplumbed) house in

Achmelvich; 'A voice of summer', which was the voice of the corncrake in the hayfield by the house and 'Toad'. Toads often entered the Achmelvich house.

The croft house next door was occupied by Pollóchan (the croft name) and family. Pollóchan was one of the many Donald MacLeods in the area. He was a traditional crofter, keeping sheep, cows and hens and selling milk from the front door. He was a generous friend of the McCaigs and, in his quiet way, a man of some distinction. The croft appears in many poems, such as 'Fetching cows', and 'Byre'. Pollóchan himself makes many appearances, though often unnamed. He is 'sauntering Orpheus' in 'Running bull', written in 1981 some thirty years after the event (which I witnessed as a boy); he is the unnamed companion in 'Haymaking'; he is the unnamed person in 'Crofter'.

Inverkirkaig was the base for more extensive fishing expeditions in newly explored landscapes. There are numerous poems featuring the River Kirkaig and its locality. It was also the home of 'A. K.' MacLeod whose life is celebrated and death lamented in 'Poems for Angus'. Angus worked maintaining the road running south from Inverkirkaig towards Achiltibuie, but that was his least significant attribute. He was a man of great social charm, humour and humanity and with a profound knowledge of the local land and wildlife. Angus and Pollóchan feature very much more in MacCaig's poetry than any other person. Normally, my father was reluctant to write about individuals, especially those close to him, so his poetic treatment of these men is exceptional, especially with Angus. In addition to the personal love and respect that my father had for these friends I believe that he experienced them partly as symbolic figures, representing all that he felt was best and most characteristic about the Assynt people. They were people whose friendship he aspired to.

My father's poetic response to Assynt was not immediate. A few poems were written in the 1950s but significant numbers did not appear until he had been an annual visitor for over fifteen years. They then grew in frequency and, when age and infirmity took over and he could no longer go there, more and more of his work drew on Assynt. Time was usually needed: apparently minor events become poems decades later. The response to Assynt was not a facilely descriptive one. Almost no poetry was written when he was in Assynt. This was partly because it was crowded out by other activities but mainly because this was a time for refuelling. The poetry came later.

It is worth considering where the special quality in the Assynt work came from. Assynt is a beautiful place with nice people in it, but that does not fully explain the depth of personal and poetic engagement in the poetry. I do not believe that his poetic talent was all he brought to Assynt. What he brought there, in my perception, was the impact of his childhood holidays in Scalpay, Harris, the birthplace of his mother. These happy visits made an indelible impression on him, of the place and, especially, of the people and his own heritage. His Scalpay poems are not very numerous, but they are among his finest.

Despite being family and a welcome guest in Scalpay, he was an English speaker and, for lack of a softer word, an outsider. Without implying the least unhappiness, I believe this stayed with him all his life, as profound childhood impressions do, and gave him a longing for acceptance in the Assynt community that could never be fully assuaged by the reality of the friendships he found there. This was visible in company. In Edinburgh social gatherings he was normally centre stage, where he tended to dictate the topics of conversation and generally take charge. In Assynt he was no less gregarious, but he became more of a listener and he looked up to the company in a way that would have been inconceivable elsewhere.

His Scalpay visits were of fundamental importance in bringing him to Assynt in the first place. He had extensive knowledge of the Highlands, gained as a young man when he went for lengthy cycling and camping holidays with friends, covering virtually everywhere, both on and off road, on a single gear bicycle. These travels put Assynt into a context, when, following the war and the appearance of young children, he drew on this knowledge of Scotland when selecting a place for family holidays. Achmelvich was chosen. It was ideal for children and good for fishing, but other places will have suited in such ways. He said that a major factor in the choice was a similarity in the Assynt coastal landscape to Scalpay and the east of Harris. He was, in a sense, seeking his roots. Scalpay itself would have been unthinkable by this time – too minister-ridden, too teetotal and even further away from Edinburgh.

In selecting Assynt his instincts guided him well. A more fertile soil for planting the seedlings that had been germinating since childhood could not have been found, and the fruit was many great poems. It brought him happiness, but without stultifying contentment. He had to 'woo the mountain, till I know the meaning of the meaning, no less', a process that kept him writing Assynt poems into his eighties, with no loss of freshness.

Ewen McCaig, 2018

INTRODUCTION

'Landscape and I get on together well,' said the poet, and here's the proof.

Norman MacCaig's wry love of the created world, and all its creatures, illuminates his poetry. Wherever he found himself, in line after line, he shows us how 'hieroglyphs of light fade one by one / But re-create themselves, their message done, / For ever and ever.' ('Landscape and I'.) But it was among the mountains, lochs and shores of his beloved Assynt that this vision achieved its fullest expression, and the poems in this selection are testimony to that.

   In discussion with Ewen, we agreed to limit our choice of poems to those that made specific references to Assynt, although we know that others will have sprung from that source, too. Ewen remembers, after all, that his father wrote in retrospect, back in Edinburgh, after long summers in the rugged landscape he loved so much. We also agreed to keep the poems broadly in the order of their composition, from the 1950s to the 1990s, (signalled by the titled subsections) so that readers might follow the poet's changing relationship, over more than forty years, to both the place and his own art. For Ewen this was an act of shared experience, because he remembers drinking from 'Vestey's well' on one of his father's fishing routes, and the day the Achmelvich transformer was 'Struck by lightning', not to mention the actual toad of

'Toad', and the sea fishing in Pollóchan's boat, the very one that features in 'Praise of a boat' and 'Basking shark'.

In early poems such as 'Dying landscape' and 'Inverkirkaig Bay' we see traces of the poet's almost metaphysical engagement with the strangeness of being, and the challenge of putting that experience, or indeed any experience, into words: 'Such clarity of seeming can declare / More than my utter self to me, who say / In clouds of words less than that false cloud there.' ('Inverkirkaig Bay'.) Soon, however, a new voice emerges, plainer, more human and more humorous, but no less engaged with the play between words and the living world around us. Ewen recalls the old tap by the roadside, where they fetched water for the Achmelvich house, but 'Water tap' brings us to a transcendental moment, expressed in the very simplest language: 'You laughed by the fence; / And everything that was / Hoisting water / Suddenly spilled over.' Many of the finest poems from these years use rhyme, often with only two rhyming lines set within a four-line stanza, but 'Water tap' is an early example of the poet's distinctive use of unrhymed verse, before he moved almost exclusively to free verse in the mid to late 1960s.

The rather painterly titles chosen by MacCaig ('A corner of the road, early morning', 'By Achmelvich bridge', 'Looking down on Glen Canisp', 'Summer evening in Assynt') speak for his strong visual sense, but they are equally rich with sounds and smell ('the hill burn's voice . . . the scent of thyme and bog myrtle'), along with the natural world of ravens, deer, fish, frogs and movement – always movement – including the movement of his own creative mind:

> The mosses on the wall
> Plump their fat cushions up. They smell of wells,
> Of under bridges and of spoons. They move
> More quiveringly than the dazed rims of bells.

("By Achmelvich bridge')

The poet's engagement with Assynt went beyond the considerable pleasures of friendship and fishing, and the subsection titled 'the misty landscape of history' signals this in three poems from the mid '60s and 1971, which are much longer than MacCaig's usual lyric span. 'A man in Assynt' was written for a BBC television programme in 1967, and it adds a historical and political perspective to his own deeply personal relationship with the place: 'Who possesses this landscape? – / The man who bought it or / I who am possessed by it?' By far the longest poem MacCaig ever wrote, at 274 lines, 'A man in Assynt' begins with geological time and goes on to reflect on how this land has fared, not always happily, subject to clan warfare, religious strife, the Clearances, depopulation, and modern tourism. Yet somehow it has endured, stony, intractable, rich with weather, animals, spectacular scenery and the life of the hardy folk who remain there. The poet would have cheered when the Assynt Crofters' Trust succeeded in buying back 21,000 acres from Lord Vestey in 1992, allowing the people who live and work on the land to have some control over their own economic future.

The poem 'No end, no beginning' takes four sections to reflect on the treasures that the world, and especially the landscape of Assynt, has brought to the poet, and how he translates those treasures into poetry:

> On the track to Fewin I met
> heaped hills – a still-life of enormous apples:
> and an owl swivelling his face like a plate
> in a fir tree: and a grassgreen beetle
> like a walking brooch.
>
> All themselves and all likenesses.

– and then this bounty turns into a turbulent celebration of continuity, unity and creative transformation, including, unusually for MacCaig, a love poem to 'your face, / girl in my mind', along with gulls, dinghies and blades of grass, all in 'such a web of likenesses'. The third of these longer poems, 'Centre of centres', sees the poet on Lochinver Pier, thinking about identity and how he seems divided between the man who lives and works in Edinburgh, with its own ancient history, and the figure who is possessed by the wild land and the clatter and clutter of the fishing boats and herring gulls around him: 'How many geometries are there / with how many circles / to be a centre of?' The same sense of being 'Two men at once' features in that much later poem, written when he could no longer visit the Highlands, living in the city and yet somehow still back at the Culag bar, or fishing in the Veyatie burn, 'cutting the pack of memories / and turning up ace after ace after ace.'

The Assynt poems show how MacCaig's engagement with the community developed over the years, although, as Ewen remembers, he was content simply to be accepted and to grow slow friendships there, without any need to take centre stage. The poem 'Among scholars' has a deep respect for men like Charlie Ross, the head gamekeeper who can 'read the landscape as / I read a book'. Angus Macleod features in this poem, too, and the finely understated elegiac verses in 'Poems for Angus' speak very movingly of MacCaig's close friendship with 'A. K.': and darkly, too, for that sense of evanescence – now suddenly personal – that lies behind the celebration of life and beauty in all lyric poetry:

> I look at the estuary and see
> a gravel bank and a glitter going through it
> and the stealthy tide, black-masked
> drowning stone after stone.

> ('From his house door')

This sustained sequence of twelve poems, again, an unusual format for the poet, confirms the strength of his ties to the place and its people.

Further intimations of mortality begin to colour some of the Assynt poems from the mid 1980s. There were other losses in the poet's life, after all, including his old friend Christopher Grieve in 1978, and, well into his seventies himself, MacCaig was visiting the North West more in memory than in person. A poem such as 'On the pier at Kinlochbervie' recognises a moment of existential anguish and separation in which physical, mental and creative distances seem equally oppressive:

> That fishing boat is a secret
> approaching me. It's a secret
> coming out of another one.
> I want to know the first one of all.
>
> Everything's in the distance,
> as I am. I wish I could flip that distance
> like a cigarette into the water.

The scythe in 'A man walking through Clachtoll' is recognised as an ironic symbol, invisible to the young man who carries it, but not quite so innocent to the older poet: 'And the hay falls and the dances end. / And the scythe cuts, no matter who's holding it.' In the last poem of this selection, written two years after his wife Isabel died in 1990, MacCaig reflects on life and his own creativity:

> An obstinate old rowan tree
> stands on a tiny island.
> So many storms, yet there it is
> with only a few berries, each determined
> to be the last one to drop into the water.

> ('By the Three Lochans')

The poem recalls those thorn bush images from earlier years, in which a much younger poet, angular and not exactly unprickly himself, found humorous kinship with an old rosebush located, according to Ewen, at a bend of the road above Achmelvich. ('A corner of the road, early morning'; 'Old rose bush'; 'Praise of a thorn bush'.) Even so, these sometimes melancholic later poems never lose touch with the energy and delight of the world and the memories they bring to life again. Such is the power of MacCaig's poetry, that those memories have become ours, too.

> When the salt gales drag through you
> you whip them with flowers
> and I think –
> Exclamations for you, little rose bush,
> and a couple of fanfares.

('Praise of a thorn bush')

'LONG JOURNEY BACK'

Back to Sutherland after a long absence

We'll pitch a tent in one past self
After another. Lochs will be lies,
The sky like an old nurse will babble
And mountains stand round in pretence.

Fictitious Nows will soak our shoulders,
Jump from our motor tyres, hold out
Over dark and scrabbled counters
Bacon and tea and cigarettes.

Now won't be there except for moments.
And you at the steering wheel will sit
Not knowing that on the seat beside you
Is a bundle of old and lively ghosts.

Long journey back, but never over.
One to make it, so many there.
So many faces to say, 'A stranger.
Why does he stop like that and stare?'

March 1950

Inverkirkaig Bay

Colour is comment of the cheating eye.
This bay, these islands walk themselves away
(When I have put my lust of looking by
And sink unnoticed into my natural gray)
To an odd world where senses never pry.

Even shape that advertises any man
Is lies to let us know him. That woman there,
Black on the steep road down to Badnaban,
Carts a whole fiction with her through the air
Whose shape's its title, reading 'Katie Ann'.

The seatrout nosing in along the shore
Taste the fresh water and the spawning beds.
They leap from their world into this, explore
A hidden sense of themselves and drive their heads
Into a knowledge they've not had before.

Sunrise and moonrise quietly get on
With their true miracles, which are never seen
For these explosions that we dote upon.
The roedeer hides in more than the bracken's green,
And round the stone gathers the sheltering stone.

But such a green, and such a shape in air
That with blunt fists boxes the sea away!
Such clarity of seeming can declare
More than my utter self to me, who say
In clouds of words less than that false cloud there.

September 1956

[4]

Climbing Suilven

I nod and nod to my own shadow and thrust
A mountain down and down.
Between my feet a loch shines in the brown,
Its silver paper crinkled and edged with rust.
My lungs say No;
But down and down this treadmill hill must go.

Parishes dwindle. But my parish is
This stone, that tuft, this stone
And the cramped quarters of my flesh and bone.
I claw that tall horizon down to this;
And suddenly
My shadow jumps huge miles away from me.

March 1954

Swimming lizard

He swam through the cool loch water
As though not knowing whether he slanted down
Or up to the brightness. Swimming was all he did.

The tiny monster, the alligator
A finger long, swam unhurried through the brown;
Each eye glittered under its heavy lid.

This was his witness and his protest,
To swim unhurried; for an unknown Cause
He twinkled his brief text through the brown and still.

And I, like it, too big to be noticed,
Hung over him in pity, and my help, too, was
No reaching hand, but a loving and helpless will.

June 1952

Maiden Loch

In the round bay a drifting boat
Rides on another's shadowy back
And unreflecting lilies float,
Whose whiteness makes brown water black.

Beyond the point, where islands are,
A black-throat diver wails and, there,
Making his own bill his Pole star,
Paddles himself into the air.

The glinting rod-tip bends and with
A customary brief struggle life
Gives in to a more lasting myth.
An oar-blade flashes like a knife.

The Minch breathes once across the land
And till that breathing dies away
Tall reeds stiffly whisper and
Gravely lean over all one way.

March 1954

Haycock, Achiltibuie

Tanned in a solstice, fighting mackerel
In air half shore, half sea, it dwindles daily
To a hank of grass-hair, from a sopping hay-hill.

Hay-sweet, brine-salt, the air that bleaches it
Crisscrosses its fingers like a fan and salty
Flavours are tasted in the too honey-sweet.

It sinks into itself from blond to blond,
Wrecked on pure haycock, all its fat blades stranded.
Some saints, too, smelled of honey when they died.

A sort of holiness has been cut down
And heaped up in one hill, with many mansions
Where mice, its little sinners, can run in.

Till comes the wintry crofter, hoisting half
A Zion on his back, and pitiful
Small angels fall through nights and days of frost.

And even the crofter, shrugging by his fire,
Snug in his shaking house, will look up, hearing
Such execrations battering at his door.

December 1956

Goat

The goat, with amber dumb-bells in his eyes,
The blasé lecher, inquisitive as sin,
White sarcasm walking, proof against surprise,

The nothing like him goat, goat-in-itself,
Idea of goatishness made flesh, pure essence
In idle masquerade on a rocky shelf –

Hangs upside down from lushest grass to twitch
A shrivelled blade from the cliff's barren chest,
And holds the grass well lost; the narrowest niche

Is frame for the devil's face; the steepest thatch
Of barn or byre is pavement to his foot;
The last, loved rose a prisoner to his snatch;

And the man in his man-ness, passing, feels suddenly
Hypocrite found out, hearing behind him that
Vulgar vibrato, thin derisive me-eh.

November 1956

'ENVIABLE LANDSCAPES'

Memory two ways

Along a road, all corners,
Into whose deepest secret
The huge Atlantic pokes
One of its crooked fingers,

Through tunnels damp with rowans,
Past Loch an Ordain, winking
With islands in its eye,
One of my selves is going

Ten years ago. Ten summers
Have quenched their flowery bonfire,
Ten winters have flamed white,
And there he is, dark figure,

A fact for time to curse at,
Sending on to my envy
A sky green as an egg
And two capsizing ravens

And moist ferns in a gully
And the sound of slapstick water
Perpetually falling downstairs.
If he could see his fellow,

His ten years older brother,
How many roads, all corners,
He'd have to look along
To find him here, dark figure

In enviable landscapes
Where space is of all meanings
And clownish times fall down
To beautiful Atlantics

Whose presence, breathing inland,
Enriches all it breathes on
With trembling atmospheres,
With sounds becoming soundless.

From *A Round of Applause*
(mostly 1959–61)

Sound of the sea on a still evening

It comes through quietness, softly crumbling in
Till it becomes the quietness; and we know
The wind to be will reach us from Loch Roe.
From the receding South it will begin
To stir, to whisper; and by morning all
The sea will lounge North, sloping by Clachtoll.

Gentlest of prophecies. The most tottering grass
Stands still as a stiff thorn, as though its root
Groped not in sand but in sand's absolute
And was itself disqualified to pass
Into a shaking world where it must be
Not grass but grasses rippling like the sea.

Three heifers slouch by, trailing down the road
A hundred yards of milky breath – they rip
The grasses sideways. Waterdrops still drip
From the turned tap and tinily explode
On their flat stone. An unseen bird goes by,
Its little feathers hushing the whole sky.

And yet a word is spoken. When the light
Gives back its redness to the Point of Stoer
And sets off cocks like squibs, pebbles will roar
At their harsh labour, grinding shells to white
And glittering beaches, and tall waves will run
Fawning on rocks and barking in the sun.

From A Round of Applause
(mostly 1959–61)

Spraying sheep

Old tufts of wool lie on the grass.
The clipping's over. But once again
The small quicksilver flock come pouring
Down from the hill towards the pen.

Dogs coax them to the roofless steading.
They bunch, plunge forward, one by one.
When half's outside and half within, they
Make a white hourglass in the sun.

The dogs run on the ruined walls,
Swinging their tongues, their minds all sheep.
The zinc bath winks, the stirrup pump
Guzzles the primrose one foot deep.

Then out they come, bounding high over
Nothing at all, and ramble on
The shining grass – not quicksilver
But golden fleeces, every one.

From *A Round of Applause*
(mostly 1959–61)

Culag Pier

A moderate jargon – winches, cries in Gaelic,
Cordage against the sky: most moderate when
A gull slews in with icefloes in his eyes
And a seal of crimson dapper on his beak;
A frosty distance follows where he flies.

Yet see him, pick-and-run, as he hauls a herring
Through slats of a fishbox, ululating oaths
In a sort of Eskimo at whatever stands
Between his greed and his belly – see him swerving
Out of infinity, steered by guts and glands.

The moderate jargon takes the two things in –
The winged etcetera in his etcetera wastes
Or small town gangster pillaging a slum –
And, puffing incense of brine and oily iron,
Jubilates briskly of its kingdom come.

The moderation is, of course, no mask.
Grace is hilarity; and this scene has
Good nature, in two meanings, as its meaning,
Where a transcendence feeds on guts and makes
No bones of it, nor thinks it worth the screening.

And the observing mind, in its own sun,
Takes it as so. Fishboxes swing between
The darkness and the light and herrings go

Where they could not have guessed in their broad ocean,
And ropes seem tangled, but they are not so.

From *A Round of Applause*
(mostly 1959–61)

Midnight, Lochinver

Wine-coloured, Homer said, wine-dark . . .
The seaweed on the stony beach,
Flushed darker with that wine, was kilts
And beasts and carpets . . . A startled heron
Tucked in its cloud two yellow stilts.

And eiderducks were five, no, two –
No, six. A lounging fishbox raised
Its broad nose to the moon. With groans
And shouts the steep burn drowned itself;
And sighs were soft among the stones.

All quiet, all dark: excepting where
A cone of light stood on the pier
And in the circle of its scope
A hot winch huffed and puffed and gnashed
Its iron fangs and swallowed rope.

The nursing tide moved gently in.
Familiar archipelagos
Heard her advancing, heard her speak
Things clear, though hard to understand
Whether in Gaelic or in Greek.

From *A Round of Applause*
(mostly 1959–61)

High up on Suilven

Gulfs of blue air, two lochs like spectacles,
A frog (this height) and Harris in the sky –
There are more reasons for hills
Than being steep and reaching only high.

Meeting the cliff face, the American wind
Stands up on end: chute going the wrong way.
Nine ravens play with it and
Go up and down its lift half the long day.

Reasons for them? the hill's one . . . A web like this
Has a thread that goes beyond the possible;
The old spider outside space
Runs down it – and where's raven? Or where's hill?

From *A Round of Applause*
(mostly 1959–61)

Moorings

In a salt ring of moonlight
The dinghy nods at nothing.
It paws the bright water
And scatters its own shadow
In a false net of light.

A ruined chain lies reptile,
Tied to the ground by grasses.
Two oars, wet with sweet water
Filched from the air, are slanted
From a wrecked lobster creel.

The cork that can't be travels –
Nose of a dog otter.
It's piped at, screamed at, sworn at
By an elegant oystercatcher
On furious orange legs.

With a sort of idle swaying
The tide breathes in. Harsh seaweed
Uncrackles to its kissing;
The skin of the water glistens;
Rich fat swims on the brine.

And all night in his stable
The dinghy paws bright water,
Restless steeplechaser

Longing to clear the hurdles
That ring the Point of Stoer.

From *A Round of Applause*
(mostly 1959–61)

Poachers, early morning

The net was spread upon the ground.
As though a sort of cloud it lay
Where fish had failed to fly. They cleaned
Their choking cloud, their Milky Way
Whose constellations bulged in sacks
Soon to be heaved upon their backs.

Enlarged in the enlarging light,
Two bustling primitives, they shook
A sixty yards long diagram out;
Four huge deft hands reached out and took
Precisely knots of weed and wrack,
The smooth, the varicose, the black.

Centuries, generations made
A natural ritual of a crime
And with their less than human hand
Lifted two rascals out of time
Till, each his own ancestor, they
Carried their holy spoils away.

From *A Round of Applause*
(mostly 1959–61)

Byre

The thatched roof rings like heaven where mice
Squeak small hosannahs all night long,
Scratching its golden pavements, skirting
The gutter's crystal river-song.

Wild kittens in the world below
Glare with one flaming eye through cracks,
Spurt in the straw, are tawny brooches
Splayed on the chests of drunken sacks.

The dimness becomes darkness as
Vast presences come mincing in,
Swagbellied Aphrodites, swinging
A silver slaver from each chin.

And all is milky, secret, female.
Angels are hushed and plain straws shine.
And kittens miaow in circles, stalking
With tail and hindleg one straight line.

From *A Round of Applause*
(mostly 1959–61)

Water tap

There was this hayfield,
You remember, pale gold
If it weren't hazed
With a million clover heads.

A rope of water
Frayed down – the bucket
Hoisted up a plate
Of flashing light.

The thin road screwed
Into hills; all ended
Journeys were somewhere,
But far, far.

You laughed, by the fence;
And everything that was
Hoisting water
Suddenly spilled over.

From *A Round of Applause*
(mostly 1959–61)

Loch Sionascaig

Hard to remember how the water went
Shaking the light,
Until it shook like peas in a riddling plate.

Or how the islands snored into the wind,
Or seemed to, round
Stiff, plunging headlands that they never cleared.

Or how a trout hung high its drizzling bow
For a count of three –
Heraldic figure on a shield of spray.

Yet clear the footprint in the puddled sand
That slowly filled
And rounded out and smoothed and disappeared.

From *A Round of Applause*
(mostly 1959–61)

July evening

A bird's voice chinks and tinkles
Alone in the gaunt reedbed –
   Tiny silversmith
Working late in the evening.

I sit and listen. The rooftop
With a quill of smoke stuck in it
   Wavers against the sky
In the dreamy heat of summer.

Flowers' closing time: bee lurches
Across the hayfield, singing
   And feeling its drunken way
Round the air's invisible corners.

And grass is grace. And charlock
Is gold of its own bounty.
   The broken chair by the wall
Is one with immortal landscapes.

Something has been completed
That everything is part of,
   Something that will go on
Being completed forever.

From *A Round of Applause*
(mostly 1959–61)

A voice of summer

In this one of all fields I know the best
All day and night, hoarse and melodious, sounded
A creeping corncrake, coloured like the ground,
Till the cats got him and gave the rough air rest.

Mechanical August, dowdy in the reeds,
He ground his quern and the round minutes sifted
Away in the powdery light. He would never lift
His beady periscope over the dusty hayseeds.

Cunning low-runner, tobogganing on his breast
He slid from sight once, from my feet. He only
Became the grass; then stone scraped harsh on stone,
Boxing the compass round his trivial nest.

– Summer now is diminished, is less by him.
Something that it could say cannot be spoken –
As though the language of a subtle folk
Had lost a word that had no synonym.

February 1962

No accident

Walking downhill from Suilven (a fine day, for once)
I twisted a knee. Two crippling miles to walk.
Leap became lower. Bag swung from a bowed neck.
Pedant of walking learned it like a dunce.

I didn't mind so much. Suilven's a place
That gives more than a basket of trout. It opens
The space it lives in and a heaven's revealed, in glimpses.
Grace is a crippling thing. You've to pay for grace.

The heaven's an odd one, shaped like cliff and scree
No less than they are: no picnicking place, but hiding
Forevers and everywhere in every thing – including
A two-mile walk, even, and a crippled knee.

You reach it by revelation. Good works can't place
Heaven in a dead hind and a falcon going
Or in the hard truth that, if only by being
First in a lower state, you've to pay for grace.

February 1962

Signs and signals

The Loch of the Wolf's Pass
And the Loch of the Green Corrie
Are both hung high in the air.
Rock, sphagnum and grass

Set them there. They shine
With the drenched light of the sky.
Round them the deer: and, over,
An eagle rules its line

Straight for its nest, midge-speck
On a ledge of Ben More Assynt –
Ptarmigan crouch in the stones . . .
Now the hinds move off, on trek

To Glen Coul; they unhurriedly wind
Round the Loch of the Green Corrie
And the Loch of the Wolf's Pass
That are hung there in my mind

And drenched with meaning – where the high
Eagle tears apart
The wind, and the ptarmigan, each
A stone with a crimson eye,

Crouch on my self's ground.
The water rocks, and the meaning
Tilts to its brighter self
And flashes all worlds around –

I see them jump in the air,
They wheel in the tall cathedral
Where space tumbles before
The altar of everywhere.

September 1962

Fire water

The water was still, dead black.
In it comets shot off
From the drifting boat, their track
Ten yards of greenish fire.

Corks bobbed. Arms plunged in
And were arms of fire. They plunged
Through the black water-skin
To a boiling cloud of fire.

From the fiery cloud they plucked
A salmon, cold as a saint.
Clout him. Stuff him in the rucked
Neck of the slimy sack.

Two fires quenched . . . The boat
Crept off, with a string of fire
Trailed thinly round its throat
And comets under its keel.

October 1962

Sandstone mountain

The bare rock hill turned out to be
A rocky sponge – it leaked all round
A maze of trickles. There's a broad shelf that is
A lace of them. Deer love it. No-one can see
Them couched there on the plumped and quilted ground
Except by being half raven. Let a bullet miss,
It crosses gulfs: cliffs clip back the short sound.

Of any place, a place to see
Light being water, quirking down.
Half raven, in my feathers, I was there.
Hinds raised their heads in V's. They stood to me
In bonny broadside, then moved off, a brown
Cloud going. The hill streamed ribbons everywhere,
Perpetual conjuror, from his sandstone gown.

October 1962

Bull

Black bull denies
The world is bright. He tramples
It to his own blackness
And burns it with his eyes.

Space yields, rebuffed
By him in this order:
Head's box, body's barrel,
Pinched haunches – tail's tuft.

Caged in his cage,
He dwarfs the dyke he smoulders
By; is a cloud of thunder.
He moans, with lust and rage –

Black Jove, on fire,
Locked in his ruinous heaven
From the sauntering filmstar heifer
Mincing towards the byre.

February 1962

Sheep dipping, Achmelvich

The sea goes flick-flack or the light does. When
John chucks the ewe in, she splays up two wings
That beat once and are water once again.

Pushing her nose, she trots slow-motion through
The glassy green. The others bleat and plunge –
If she must do it, what else is there to do?

They leap from ledges, all legs in the air
All furbelows and bulged eyes in the green
Turned suds, turned soda with the plumping there.

They haul themselves ashore. With outraged cries
They waterfall uphill, spread out and stand
Dribbling salt water into flowers' eyes.

November 1962

By Achmelvich bridge

Night stirs the trees
With breathings of such music that they sway,
Skirts, sleeves, tiaras, in the humming dark,
Their highborn heads tossing in disarray.

A floating owl
Unreels his silence, winding in and out
Of different darknesses. The wind takes up
And scatters a sound of water all about.

No moon need slide
Into the sky to make that water bright;
It ties its swelling self with glassy ropes;
It jumps from stones in smithereens of light.

The mosses on the wall
Plump their fat cushions up. They smell of wells,
Of under bridges and of spoons. They move
More quiveringly than the dazed rims of bells.

A broad cloud drops
A darker darkness. Turning up his stare,
Letting the world pour under him, owl goes off,
His small soft foghorn quavering through the air.

November 1962

A corner of the road, early morning

The thorny light
Scratched out a lanky rose bush in the air.
Goats had been at it, leaving five flowers there.

Scrabbles of bright
Water ran linking down the pink road. Pink
Rocks shouldered it to the left. The ditch ran ink.

I felt the night
Inside my head, like the one outside it, fade
Till its last shadow swallowed its last shade.

And into sight
Of inner as of outer eye there grew
Shapes into shape, colours becoming true.

By holding tight
To loosing every hold, I began to see
What I was not helping myself to be.

I looked up: white
Against a blue – five suns. And this I wrote
Beneath the constellation of the Goat.

November 1962

Remembering old Murdo scything

A place where sand
Drifts white on the road
And the knees of the Split Rock
Are frilled with white water.

Curved back, claw hands
Bring more to the ground
Than walls of grass.
They scythe a whole city.

Edinburgh falls flat.
Its swathes of streets
Jump with grasshoppers
And clover petals.

And a spurred hawk rides
Bareback on the wind
Whose cantering makes
Bright water brighter.

December 1962

Struck by lightning

The tall transformer stood
Biblically glorified, and then turned blue.
Space split. The earth tossed twelve hens in the air.
The landscape's hair stood up. The collie flew,
Or near it, back to the house and vanished there.

Roofed by a gravel pit,
I, in a safe place, as I always am,
Was, as I always am, observer only
– Nor cared. Why should I? The belief's a sham
That shared danger or escape cures being lonely.

Yet when I reached the croft
They excluded me by telling me. As they talked
Across my failure, I turned away to see
Hills spouting white and a huge cloud that walked
With a million million legs on to the sea.

February 1963

Winter

Shepherds, tramping the frozen bogland
Beside the sheeted ghost of Quinag,
Hear guns go off in the shrivelling air –
Not guns, ice on the frozen lochans
Whose own weight is too gross to bear.

Crofter, coughing in the morning,
Sees the pale window crossed with branches
Of a new tree. He wipes a rag
Across the glass and, there, a beggar
In his own tatters, a royal stag.

Six black stumps on the naked skerry
Draw the boat close in. The oarsman,
Feeling a new cold in his bones,
Sees cormorants, glazed to the sea-rock,
Carved out of life, their own tombstones.

May 1963

Among scholars

On our way to a loch, two miles from Inveruplan,
Three of us (keepers) read the landscape as
I read a book. They missed no word of it:
Fox-hole, strange weed, blue berry, ice-scrape, deer's hoof-print.
It was their back yard, and fresh as the garden in Eden
(Striped rock 'like a Belted Galloway'). They saw what I
Saw, and more, and its meaning. They spoke like a native
The language they walked in. I envied them, naturally.

Coming back, we dragged the boat down to Inveruplan,
Lurching and slithering, both it and us. A stag
Paused in the thickening light to see that strange thing,
A twelve-legged boat in a bog. Angie roared at it
Like a stag in rut. Denying its other senses
It came and paused and came – and took itself off,
A text, a chapter and verse, into its gospel.
We took up the rope and hauled on, sweating and gasping.

We left the boat in the hayfield at Inveruplan:
The tractor would get it. A moon was coming up
Over the roof and under it a Tilley lamp
Hissed in its yellow self. We took our noise
Into the room and shut it in with us
Where, till light broke on a boat foundered in dew,
I drank down drams in a company of scholars
With exploding songs and a three-days ache in my shoulder.

September 1963

Fetching cows

The black one, last as usual, swings her head
And coils a black tongue round a grass-tuft. I
Watch her soft weight come down, her split feet spread.

In front, the others swing and slouch; they roll
Their great Greek eyes and breathe out milky gusts
From muzzles black and shiny as wet coal.

The collie trots, bored, at my heels, then plops
Into the ditch. The sea makes a tired sound
That's always stopping though it never stops.

A haycart squats prickeared against the sky.
Hay breath and milk breath. Far out in the West
The wrecked sun founders though its colours fly.

The collie's bored. There's nothing to control . . .
The black cow is two native carriers
Bringing its belly home, slung from a pole.

October 1963

Falls pool, evening

The level blaze poured up the Kirkaig gorge
Straight from the sun, projecting technicolour
Rowan berries and birch bark and bell heather
On the dripping crags. Keeping its restless place,
A pillar of flies juggled itself in space.

Eight feet by two. Downstream another one
And then another stood in the powerful brightness –
Nebulas, distaffs, fiery figures, weightless
As the thick light that they were fiery in.
They kept their shape however they might spin.

Up from the drumming water (salmon curved
In a torque of silver from one hand) we clambered
To the stalker's path and, pausing there, remembered
And looked in the fiery furnace down below
At Shadrach, Meshach and Abednego.

October 1963

Vestey's well

We raised the lid. The cold spring water was
So clear it wasn't there.
At the foot of its non-depth a grave toad squatted
As still as Buddha in his non-place. Flaws
Breathed on the water – he trembled to no-where
Then steadied into being again. A fretted
Fern was his Bo-tree. Time in that delicate place
Sat still for ever staring in its own face.

We filled the jam-jar with bright nothing and
Drank down its freezing light
That the sun burned us with (that raging planet
That will not stand and will not understand)
And tried to feel we were each one a bright
And delicate place with a philosopher in it –
And failed; and let the hinged lid slowly fall.
The little Buddha hadn't moved at all.

November 1963

Two shepherds

Donald roared and ran and brandished
his stick and swore
in all the languages
he knew, which were
some.

Pollóchan sauntered, stood
six feet three silent: with a small
turn of the hand
he'd send the collie flowing
round the half-mile-long arc
of a towsy circle.

Two poets –
Dionysian,
Apollonian
and the sheep in the pen.

June 1964

Waiting to notice

I sprawl among seapinks – a statue
fallen from the ruins
of the air into
the twentieth century – and think:
a crowd of fancies is not so easily come by
as you suppose. They have to happen
like weather, or a migration, or a haystack
going up in flames all on its own
half way through some time or other.
When they happen, the mind alerts itself –
it's as if this landscape were suddenly
to become aware
of the existence of its own elements –
possessive rock, possessing
only itself: huge lumbering sea –
that fat-fingered lacemaker who,
by sitting on shells, gives them
their shapes: mountains
reaching half way to somewhere or other:
and heather and grass and me
and a gull, as usual
tuning his bagpipe
and not going on to the tune.

Things there to be noticed.

It takes a sunshaft
to reveal the motes in the air. I wait
for that weather, that sunshaft

to show in the dark room of my mind
that invisible dancing, that
wayward and ceaseless activity, and I bend
my stone arm up till the hawk
hovering over the hayfield
perches fluttering
on my wrist.

July 1964

In this wild day

You wade through galloping grass
in this parish mythical
with Hebridean cuckoos and corn so alien
it pines for a fatter sunshine, a less
acid grip to its feet. Your raincoat
tries to go back home, but your mind,
hauling on a long purpose, pulls you,
thought over thought, to
the edge of the sea. There
you stand on a steep rock and throw
into the galloping water bottles and
tins – if they won't burn,
they'll drown. They'll rust
to a red web or glitter in the tangle
to the misunderstanding
of lobsters and congers. – But one
won't sink and, wearing itself askew,
drunkenly toddles off towards Harris.
You turn back home, with your coat
for spinnaker and the tide
of grass in your favour, to where I sit
in my snug ark, the smoke
from its streaming funnel racing
out of itself over
the slanted cornfield. From it I throw
used up ideas, empty feelings
to drown in another tide – except this one

that sidles and bobs and makes
its landfall on this
white shore.

August 1964

Above Inverkirkaig

I watch, across a loch
where seatrout are leaping,
Suilven and Cul Mor, my
mountains of mountains,
looming and pachydermatous in the thin light
of a clear half moon. Something swells
in my mind, in my self, as though
I were about to be enlarged,
to enclose informations and secrets
that lie just beyond me that I would utter
in one short, stupendous sentence, to the everlasting
benefit of mankind and landscapes and me –
a pregnant feeling that is, naturally, caused
by love.

I know, half moon-struck as I am,
the usual miscarriage will follow. I am beyond
the reach of miracles. And am glad of it,
thinking that, if this miracle were to happen
this time, it would be as if
Suilven should monstrously
move over to Cul Mor and after
coupling through human generations
drag himself back and sit
by his own lochside, indifferently
observing on the bogs of Assynt
a litter of tiny Suilvens, each one
the dead spit of his father.

October 1964

On a cloudy mountain

The shot stag runs through
more mists than one,
his lower jaw swinging loose
from burst hinges.
Let him run his fastest,
he will not outstrip
the slow death
that keeps pace with him.
For how many days
will the light darken before
his empty cage lies, growing green
on the green ground.

October 1964

Looking down on Glen Canisp

The summer air is thick, is wads
that muffle the hill burn's voice
and stifle colours
to their cloudier selves – and
bright enough: the little loch
is the one clear pane
in a stained-glass window.

The scent of thyme and bog myrtle
is so thick
one listens for it, as though it might be
a drowsy honey-hum
in the heavy air.

Even the ravens
have sunk into the sandstone cliffs
of Suilven, that are dazed blue
and fuzz into the air around them –
as my mind does, till I hear
a thin far clatter and
look down to where two stags
canter across the ford, splashing up before them
antlers of water.

December 1964

Illumination: on the track by Loch Fewin

Suddenly the sun poured
through an arrow-slit in the clouds
and the great hall we walked in – its tapestries
of mountains and parquet of rich
bogland and water – blazed on the eye
like the Book of Kells.

For four days a cloud
had sat like a lid on the round
horizon. But now
we walked in a mediaeval manuscript –
doves flew over the thorn, the serpent
of wisdom whispered
in our skulls and our hands
were transparent with love.

May 1965

Humanism

When the glacier was defeated
in the siege of Suilven and limped off
to the East, it left behind it all that
burdened its retreat –
stones, the size of
sandgrains and haystacks:
abandoned loot of Glen Canisp.

What a human lie is this. What greed and what
arrogance, not to allow
a glacier to be a glacier –
to humanise into a metaphor
that long slither of ice – that was no more
a beaten army than it was a horde
of Cinderellas, each,
when her midnight sounded,
leaving behind her
a sandstone shoe.

I defend the glacier that
when it absorbs a man
preserves his image
intact.

September 1965

Between

To think that between
those stoniest of mountains, Foinaven and
Arkle, there lies a loch
that deserves a name like –
The Loch of the Corrie of the Green Waterfalls!

Today and tomorrow are
Foinaven and Arkle, are
the barest of days.
– But tonight
she will be with me whose name
outsings in my mind
all the waterfalls in Scotland.

January 1966

Moment musical in Assynt

A mountain is a sort of music: theme
And counter theme displaced in air amongst
Their own variations.
Wagnerian Devil signed the Coigach score;
And God was Mozart when he wrote Cul Mor.

You climb a trio when you climb Cul Beag.
Stac Polly – there's a rondo in seven sharps,
Neat as a trivet.
And Quinag, rallentando in the haze,
Is one long tune extending phrase by phrase.

I listen with my eyes and see through that
Mellifluous din of shapes my masterpiece
Of masterpieces:
One sandstone chord that holds up time in space –
Sforzando Suilven reared on his ground bass.

February 1967

Small round loch

Lochan Dubh is too small
for any wind to lash it
into the vulgarity of crashing waves
and spit spray. In any storm
it finnicks amongst its reeds and pebbles
with inextinguishable preciosity – cunning
 watchmaker of light and water.
I see a jewel here, a jewel there,
small emerald, chip of diamond, minuscule
sapphire, taking the strain
of light
swivelling on water:
delicate mechanism, measuring
a time
that has no escapement.

April 1967

Old rose bush

In this salt air, the wild rose bush
is a tatter from the root up, is
a diagram from which
most lines have been erased.

With straight lines and obtuse
angles it explores
the three visible dimensions
and produces from the fourth
one rose.

It stands like a beggar
at the corner of the road –
skinny old seaman with
a parakeet on his shoulder.

                    July 1967

Basking shark

To stub an oar on a rock where none should be,
To have it rise with a slounge out of the sea
Is a thing that happened once (too often) to me.

But not too often – though enough. I count as gain
That once I met, on a sea tin-tacked with rain,
That roomsized monster with a matchbox brain.

He displaced more than water. He shoggled me
Centuries back – this decadent townee
Shook on a wrong branch of his family tree.

Swish up the dirt and, when it settles, a spring
Is all the clearer. I saw me, in one fling,
Emerging from the slime of everything.

So who's the monster? The thought made me grow pale
For twenty seconds while, sail after sail,
The tall fin slid away and then the tail.

December 1967

Dancing minister

In a one-two-three
she waltzes by, big as a brigantine.

Her tug, with a red-hot smokestack,
is short of tonnage, is short of horsepower.

She has no visible means
of propulsion. She drifts
curvaceously on
invisible swirlings and eddies.

A passing tug hails them: 'Minister,
what would St Luke think of you now?'

The parson sweats. Theology
was nothing to this.

From *A Man in My Position*
(mostly 1967–68)

Country dance

The room whirled and coloured
and figured itself with dancers.
Another gaiety seemed born of theirs
and flew as streamers
between their heads and the ceiling.

I gazed, coloured and figured,
down the tunnel of streamers –
and there, in the band, an old fiddler
sawing away in the privacy
of music. He bowed lefthanded and his right hand
was the wrong way round. Impossible.
But the jig bounced, the gracenotes
sparkled on the surface of the tune.
The odd man out, when it came to music,
was the odd man in.

There's a lesson here, I thought, climbing
into the pulpit I keep in my mind.
But before I'd said *Firstly brethren*, the tune
ended, the dancers parted, the old fiddler
took a cigarette from the pianist, stripped off
the paper and chewed the tobacco.

March 1969

Lord of Creation

At my age, I find myself
making a mountainous landscape
of the bedclothes. A movement
of knee and foot
and there's Cul Mor and a hollow
filled with Loch Sionascaig.
I watch tiny sheep stringing along
a lower slope.

Playing at God.

One day, when I go back to Assynt,
this could frighten me, this could make me
have to drive from my mind
a leg stretching out under ground, the collapse
of Cul Mor, the shedding
in every torrential direction
of Loch Sionascaig. But now
I cock up my left foot and create
Suilven. I watch myself
fishing from a rocky point.

– I think, *At my age!* – and
stretch out. My image vanishes.

God has destroyed himself again.

December 1968

Walking to Inveruplan

Glowing with answers in the aromatic dark,
I walk, so wise,
Under the final problem of lit skies.

I reach the bridge, where the road turns north to Stoer,
And there perch me
Under the final problem of a tree.

I'm in my Li Po mood. I've half a mind
To sit and drink
Until the moon, that's just arisen, should sink.

The whisky's good, it constellates. How wise
Can a man be,
I think, inside that final problem, me.

If you are short of answers, I've got them all
As clear as day . . .
I blink at the moon and put the bottle away

And then walk on (for there are miles to go
And friends to meet)
Above the final problem of my feet.

December 1967

Descent from the Green Corrie

The climb's all right, it's the descent that kills you.
Knees become fists that don't know how to clench
And thighs are strings in parallel.
Gravity's still your enemy; it drills you
With your own backbone – its love is all to wrench
You down on screes or boggy asphodel

And the elation that for a moment fills you
Beside the misty cairn's that lesser thing
A memory of it. It's not
The punishing climb, it's the descent that kills you
However sweetly the valley thrushes sing
And shadows darken with the peace they've brought.

From *A Man in My Position*
(mostly 1967–68)

So many summers

Beside one loch, a hind's neat skeleton,
Beside another, a boat pulled high and dry:
Two neat geometries drawn in the weather:
Two things already dead and still to die.

I passed them every summer, rod in hand,
Skirting the bright blue or the spitting gray,
And, every summer, saw how the bleached timbers
Gaped wider and the neat ribs fell away.

Time adds one malice to another one –
Now you'd look very close before you knew
If it's the boat that ran, the hind went sailing.
So many summers, and I have lived them too.

December 1967

'THE MISTY LANDSCAPE OF HISTORY'

A man in Assynt

Glaciers, grinding West, gouged out
these valleys, rasping the brown sandstone,
and left, on the hard rock below – the
ruffled foreland –
this frieze of mountains, filed
on the blue air – Stac Polly,
Cul Beag, Cul Mor, Suilven,
Canisp – a frieze and
a litany.

Who owns this landscape?
Has owning anything to do with love?
For it and I have a love-affair, so nearly human
we even have quarrels. –
When I intrude too confidently
it rebuffs me with a wind like a hand
or puts in my way
a quaking bog or a loch
where no loch should be. Or I turn stonily
away, refusing to notice
the rouged rocks, the mascara
under a dripping ledge, even
the tossed, the stony limbs waiting.

I can't pretend
it gets sick for me in my absence,
though I get
sick for it. Yet I love it
with special gratitude, since

it sends me no letters, is never
jealous and, expecting nothing
from me, gets nothing but
cigarette packets and footprints.

Who owns this landscape? –
The millionaire who bought it or
the poacher staggering downhill in the early morning
with a deer on his back?

Who possesses this landscape? –
The man who bought it or
I who am possessed by it?

False questions, for
this landscape is
masterless
and intractable in any terms
that are human.
It is docile only to the weather
and its indefatigable lieutenants –
wind, water and frost.
The wind whets the high ridges
and stunts silver birches and alders.
Rain falling down meets
springs gushing up –
they gather and carry down to the Minch
tons of sour soil, making bald
the bony scalp of Cul Mor. And frost
thrusts his hand in cracks and, clenching his fist,
bursts open the sandstone plates,

the armour of Suilven;
he bleeds stories down chutes and screes,
smelling of gunpowder.

Or has it come to this,
that this dying landscape belongs
to the dead, the crofters and fighters
and fishermen whose larochs
sink into the bracken
by Loch Assynt and Loch Crocach? –
to men trampled under the hoofs of sheep
and driven by deer to
the ends of the earth – to men whose loyalty
was so great it accepted their own betrayal
by their own chiefs and whose descendants now
are kept in their place
by English businessmen and the indifference
of a remote and ignorant government.

Where have they gone, the people
who lived between here and
Quinag, that tall
huddle of anvils that puffs out
two ravens into the blue and
looks down on the lochs of Stoer
where trout idle among reeds and
waterlilies – take one of them home
and smell, in a flower
the sepulchral smell of water.

Beyond Fewin lies the Veyatie Burn – fine
crossing place for deer, they trot over
with frills of water flouncing
at their knees. That water rests in Fewin
beneath the sandstone hulk
of Suilven, not knowing what's to come –
the clattering horserush down
the Kirkaig gorge, the sixty-foot
Falls . . . There are twenty-one pools
on the Kirkaig . . . Since
before empires were possible
till now, when so many have died
in their own dust,
the Kirkaig Falls have been walking backwards –
twenty-one paces up their own stream.
Salmon lie
in each of the huge footprints.
You can try to catch them –
at a price.
The man whose generations of ancestors
fished this, their own river,
can catch them still –
at a price . . .

The salmon come from the sea. I watch
its waves thumping down their glossy arches in
a soup of sand, folding over from one
end of the bay to the other.
Sandpipers, ringed plover, turnstones
play tig with these waves that
pay no heed but laboriously get on with

playing their million-finger exercises on
the keyboard of the sand.

The salmon come from the sea. Men
go out on it. The *Valhalla*, the *Golden Emblem*
come in, smoking with gulls,
from the fishing grounds of the Minch
to lie, docile, by the Culag pier.
Beneath it the joppling water
shuffles its blues and greens till they almost
waver the burly baulks away.
From the tall bows ropes reach ashore
in languid arcs, till, through rings, round
bollards, they clot and
twist themselves in savage knots.
The boats lie still with a cargo
of fish and voyages.

Hard labour can relax.
The salty smell outside, which is made up
of brine and seaweed
and fish, reaches the pub door but
is refused admittance. Here,
men in huge jerseys drink small drinks.
The thick talk
of fishing and sheep is livened
by a witty crackle of gossip
and the bitter last tale
of local politics. At ten o'clock, the barman
will stop whistling a strathspey to shout
'Time, please!' and they

will noisily trail out, injecting a guff of alcohol
into the salty smell made up
of brine and seaweed
and fish, which stretches from the pub door
all the way to America.
Whom does the sea belong to?
Fat governments? Guillemots? Or men
who steal from it what they can
to support their dying acres?

Fish from the sea, for Glasgow, London,
Edinburgh. But the land, too, sells
itself; and from these places
come people tired of a new civilisation
to taste what's left
of an old one. They outnumber
the locals – a thing
too easy to do . . . In Lochinver,
Achmelvich, Clashnessie, Clachtoll
they exchange the tyranny of the clock
for the natural rhythm of day and
night and day and night and for
the natural decorum that binds together
the fishing grounds, crofting lands
and the rough sheepruns that hoist themselves
towards the hills. They meet the people
and are not rejected. In the sweating night
London and Edinburgh fall away
under the bouncing rhythms of *Strip the Willow*
and the *Gay Gordons*, and when the lights go out
and all the goodnights are spoken, they can hear

a drunk melodeon go without staggering
along the dark road.

But the night's not over. A twinkle of light
in Strathan, Brackloch, Inveruplan, shows
where the tales are going round, tall
as the mast of the *Valhalla*, and songs are sung
by keeper, shepherd and fisherman,
each tilting his Rembrandt face in the light
and banging the chorus round, till, with a shout
he takes up his dram and drinks it down.
The Gauger of Dalmore lives again
in verses. An old song
makes history alive again,
as a rickle of stones peoples the dark theatre
of the mind with a shouting crowd and,
in the middle, MacLeod of Assynt and
his greater prisoner – Montrose.

An old song. A rickle of stones. A
name on a map.
I read on a map a name whose Gaelic means
the Battlefield of the Big Men.
I think of yelling hosts, banners,
counterattacks, deployments. When I get there,
it's ten acres, ten small acres
of boggy ground.
I feel
I am looking through the same wrong end
of the same telescope
through which I look back through time

and see
Christ, Socrates, Dante – all the Big Men
picked out, on their few acres,
clear and tiny in
the misty landscape of history.

Up from that mist crowds
the present. This day has lain long,
has dozed late, till
the church bell jerks and, wagging madly
in its salty tower, sends its voice
clanking through the sabbath drowse.
And dark minds in black clothes gather like
bees to the hive, to share
the bitter honey of the Word, to submit
to the hard judgment of a God
my childhood God would have a difficulty
in recognising.
Ten yards from the sea's surge
they sing to Him beautiful praises
that surge like the sea,
in a bare stone box built
for the worship of the Creator
of all colours and between-colours, and of
all shapes, and of the holiness
of identity and of the purifying light-stream
of reason. The sound of that praise
escapes from the stone box
and takes its place in the ordinary communion
of all sounds, that are

Being expressing itself – as it does in its continuous,
its never-ending creation of leaves,
birds, waves, stone boxes – and beliefs,
the true and the false.

These shapes; these incarnations, have their own determined
identities, their own dark holiness, their
high absurdities. See how they make
a breadth and assemblage of animals,
a perpendicularity of creatures, from where,
three thousand feet up, two ravens go by
in their seedy, nonchalant way, down to
the burn-mouth where baby mussels
drink fresh water through their beards –
or down, down still, to where the masked conger eel
goes like a gangster through
the weedy slums at the sea's foot.

Greenshank, adder, wildcat, guillemot, seatrout,
fox and falcon – the list winds through
all the crooks and crannies of this landscape, all
the subtleties and shifts of its waters and
the prevarications of its air –
while roofs fall in, walls crumble, gables
die last of all, and man becomes,
in this most beautiful corner of the land,
one of the rare animals.
Up there, the scraping light
whittles the cloud edges till, like thin bone,
they're bright with their own opaque selves. Down here,
a skinny rosebush is an eccentric jug

of air. They make me,
somewhere between them,
a visiting eye,
an unrequited passion,
watching the tide glittering backward and making
its huge withdrawal from beaches
and kilted rocks. And the mind
behind the eye, within the passion,
remembers with certainty that the tide will return
and thinks, with hope, that that other ebb,
that sad withdrawal of people, may, too,
reverse itself and flood
the bays and the sheltered glens
with new generations replenishing the land
with its richest of riches and coming, at last,
into their own again.

From *A Man in My Position*
(mostly 1967–68)

No end, no beginning

I

. . . And a moon fat as a butterball
Over the wet feathers of treetops;
Meadowsweet smelling of gray honey;
The sealoch bulged like a biceps
In a jersey sleeve of rocks . . .
When ever was there a beginning? –
Not of night and its furniture,
Its transcriptions, its cool décor;
Nor of thinking about it:
But when was there a beginning
Of this turbulent love
For a sea shaking with light
And lullabying ditchwater
And a young twig being grave
Against constellations – these –
And people, invisibly webbing
Countries and continents,
Weeping, laughing, being idle
And always, always
Moving from light to darkness and
To light: a furniture
Of what? – a transcription, a décor
Of Being, that hard abstract
Curled in the jelly of an eye
And webbed through constellations
And cities and deserts, and frayed
In the wet feathers of treetops.

2

On the track to Fewin I met
heaped hills – a still-life of enormous apples:
and an owl swivelling his face like a plate
in a fir tree: and a grassgreen beetle
like a walking brooch.

All themselves and all likenesses.

Or I peer down from a sea rock
through the sidling glass, the salty light,
and see in that downward world green Samoas
and swaying Ceylons.

Resemblance makes kinships. Your face,
girl in my mind, is the heir
of all the beautiful women there have been.
I look and dazzle with the loveliness
of women I've never known.

And your hand is as cool as moonlight
and as gentle.

Such a web of likenesses. No matter
how many times removed, I am cousin
to volcanoes and leafbuds, and the heron
devouring a frog eats a bloodbrother of
suns and gravestones.

3

When you, in your unimaginable self,
suddenly were there, shut boxes opened

and worlds flew out coloured like picture books
and full of heavy lethargies and gay dances:

when I met a tree, my old familiar, I knew
this was the first time I was meeting it;

and the birds in it singing – for the first time
I could crack the code of their jargon.

And the boredom and loneliness
in the lit rooms of monotonous streets became

terrible and pitiful – you made me a member
of the secret society of humanity.

The future that had been failing muscles,
sagging flesh, cindering eyes –

all mine, all only mine – swarmed in the air
and spread its new meaning back

into every yesterday. Flux, revolution
emerged into sense, into their own

explanations. I could understand them,
not wholly, but I could understand them

as I could know, not wholly, the meaning
of your still hand, quiet look, a way of walking

that takes you from the first garden to the future
where the apple hangs, still, on its dangerous tree.

4

The dinghy across the bay
Puts out two hands and swims
An elegant backstroke over
A depth full of images.

A gull swings round a rock,
Glides by. No feathers stir –
Dead still as a living fossil
In a geology of air.

I pick a round grassblade
And chew it. The sap breeds
A campfire, dark figures, a blackness
Full of dangerous woods.

And in that tree, that house,
That girl on the gray rocks,
That wave – in everything
A vigorous future kicks.

He'll be born, full of graves.
Greedy and angry. His screams
Will fill us with an ancient pity.
He'll lie helpless in our arms.

February 1968

Centre of centres

To call the pier a centre
I sit in a centre –
of cloud-stuffs, water lispings, a huge
charge of light and men doing things on boats
that result in fish. Yet I am, too, a centre
of roundabouts and No Entries, libraries,
streets full of cafés and the prickly stink
of burnt petrol:
an imposition of two circles
from different geometries
where a coincident stream refuses to be
the street it's coincident with
and tenements offer no ledge
to twirling, laborious ravens.

Where's my binocular vision now?
I see like a bird or a fish,
a boat with one eye a bus with the other,
a crofter left a traffic warden right:
a supermarket ghosts up
from the shallows of Loch Fewin
and round the foot of Suilven
go red deer and taxis.

The *Golden Emblem* seethes in, sidles
and with a friendly nudge stables herself
beside the *Valhalla*. Round my head
she releases a flicker of names
that come out of geography but emerge, too,

from myth – Muckle Flugga, Taransay, Sule Skerry,
the Old Man of Hoy.
– Though I know
she's been no farther off than Coigach Point
she has ringed her nets in the imagination
as well as the Minch
and brings ashore a cargo
the fishbuyers won't bid for.
– So, with my other eye, from my other centre,
I look at Edinburgh's High Street and a film
starts unwinding, spool on spool,
of caddies and clan chiefs, lords
and layabouts – in a broad daylight's midnight
desperate men
pull themselves up the Castle Rock –
a scabbard clinks: whispers curse
the scaling ladder.

So where's my binocular vision again?
How many geometries are there
with how many circles
to be a centre of?
As though a man, alive in his imagination,
trips on this stone and stumbles
on the field of the Battle of the Braes or, walking
to Murrayfield, is one of a crowd
moving in silence
to the execution of Montrose.

I name myself, I name this place, I say
I am here; and the immediacies

of the flesh and of the reports
of its five senses (I welcome them)
make their customary
miraculous declarations, from which
all else falls away. The landscapes
and histories of memory
disappear in a yellow basket
rising from the hold of the *Golden Emblem* and swooping
ashore, towsy with fishtails
(gray haddock, falseface skate, flounders
with wrong eyes – they slide into the shallow boxes
with a slip, with a slither, watched by me
and by herring gulls and blackbacks that stroll
the fringe of the crowd like policemen,
like pickpockets).

Who would guess
the thorn in the rose tree, the scandalous life
of Professor Schmaltz, the grunt
of a puffin? Who could foretell
the wave that towers in humped high
over the others? The argument from design
has as many flaws in it as there are
unpredictables
in the design.

I think of a man who talks as if trees were
virtuosities of wood, as if water
were liquid mechanisms built for holding up
swans. He speaks as if winds were
recordings of a master wind and not

unexampled discourses, as if birds
were spools of song that
they unwind.

What sort of apprentice sorcerer is he
whose inventions
have got out of hand? – For he forgets
the intrusion of the comic (see that sun, strolling over,
lordly magnifico, with a wig of cloud
slipping over one ear) – and of the tragic:
that whimsical water
lullabying in the sun can clench its fist
on the timbers it cradles.

In mid-air a gull, peering down, bowed
between its wings,
unbows itself and cackles,
trips over the cackle and floats on;
and a baby boat
comically staggering across the bay
stops for a rest in the dead centre
of teeming unpredictables.

Grassblade, cathedral, hero –
strawberry jam pot – each
is a centre
of innumerable circles. I sit in mine,
enriched by geometries

that make a plenum of more
than the three dimensions.
I sit and stare at them
with a multiple eye.

February 1971

'BACK AGAIN'

Back again, Lairg station

Into the seventh house of the stars
the train, caterpillaring between
green somewheres, huffed and
sighingly stopped. I, earth explorer,
stepped out, at my home station,
and faces I knew were not angels'
angelically greeted me. Hands gripped mine
with a forgotten hardness and I stood
saying nothing in different ways,
in a green somewhere, unable to bear
the fuschia hedge, the barrow wheels grinding
on grit, moved as by the finger of God
by the baggy trousers of the stationmaster,
by the stopped clock, by that most disobeyed
of orders, *Cross the line
by the bridge only.*

June 1972

July landing

The *Eilean Glas*, engine full ahead,
slavers through the sea, wolfishly
making for its lair
at Lochinver. It brushes aside
the sparkling splinters of water.

The day is wildernesses, all
desolate and lovely . . .
As monumental as a monument
a blonde sheltie drowsily stares
through filmstar eyelashes
at the road hemstitched on the skirt
of a mountain. Somewhere
a lamb laments
with the voice of desolation.

On the sand at Clashnessie
six sandpipers play tig
with the Minch, that
keeps casting up and withdrawing
a rinse of soiled lace infested
with sandgrains.

And round Stoer Point swirls
a typhoon of gulls and, under it, the *Eilean Glas*
grinning through the water
till it comes to rest at the pier

in a green seethe of watery
mushrooms and Catherine wheels
and the engine stops
with a clap of silence.

January 1972

Lesson

He watches a fishbox, say,
or a languid rope
or a seagull at attention.
– What's the matter with a fishbox? So
he watches a fishbox.
He tries to see just what it is.
He counts the slats it's made of –
sides, top and bottom –
and reads, in neat black letters,
Return to Lochinver. He notices
sixpences of scales, gone grubby.
And then he's stuck.
He goes off knowing
he hasn't seen the fishbox at all.

Meantime the fishbox
waits till it's night. Then
like a pterodactyl it planes
through the darkness and flies into
the sleeper's mind. It opens
and crams the sleeper inside it.
And when the hammer hits
the first nail on the head,
he wakes with a scream, he knows
what a fishbox is, he knows
what a rope is, or a seagull standing
at its horrible attention.

July 1972

Greenshank

His single note – one can't help calling it
piping, one can't help
calling it plaintive – slides droopingly down
no more than a semitone, but is filled
with an octave of loneliness, with the whole sad scale
of desolation.

He won't leave us. He keeps flying
fifty yards and perching
on a rock or a small hummock,
drawing attention to himself.
Then he calls and calls
and flies on again
in a flight
roundshouldered but dashing,
skulking yet bold.

Cuckoo, phoenix, nightingale,
you are no truer emblems
than this bird is.
He is the melancholy that flies
in the weathers of my mind,
he is the loneliness that calls to me there
in a semitone
of desolate octaves.

October 1972

Birthdays

In the earliest light of a long day
three stags stepped out from the birch wood
at Achmelvich bridge
to graze on the sweet grass
by the burn.
A gentle apparition.

Stone by stone a dam was built,
a small dam, small stone by stone.
And the water backed up, flooding
that small field.

I'll never see it again.
It's drowned forever.
But still
in the latest light of a lucky day I see
horned heads come from the thickets
and three gentle beasts innocently pacing
by that implacable water.

October 1972

The Pass of the Roaring

Such comfortless places comfort me.
Not my body but I am fed by these ravens
And I'm nourished by the drib-dab waters
That fingerling through the harsh deer grass.
The tall cliffs unstun my mind.
Thank God for a place where no history passes.

Is this ghoulish? Is it the vampire me
Or grandfathers and greatgrandfathers
Specklessly flowing my veins that bury
A hummingbird tongue in these gulfs of space
And suck from limestone with delicate greed
A delicate vintage, the blood of grace?

Books vaporise in my lightning mind.
Pennies and pounds become a tribal
Memory. Hours assert their rightness,
Escaping like doves through their cotes of clocks
And lame philosophies founder in bogs
That stink of summer in the armpit rockfolds.

There's always a returning. A cottage glows
By a dim sea and there I'll slump by the fireside –
And another grace will gather, from human
Intercommunications, a grace
Not to be distinguished from the one that broods
In fingerling waters and gulfs of space.

From *The World's Room*
(mostly 1972–73)

In everything

Once I was on a cliff, on a ledge of seapinks,
Contemplating nothing – it was a self-sufficient day
With not a neurotic nerve to zigzag in the blue air.
Was that happiness? (Yes.) I sat, still as a shell,
Over water, in space, amongst spiders in chinks.

But suddenly I was introduced to suddenness.
As though a train entered a room, a headlong pigeon
Cometed past me, and space opened in strips
Between pinions and tail feathers of the eagle after it –
It had seen me. What vans of brakes! What voluptuousness!

What a space in space, carved like an eagle,
It left behind it! Below me the green sea-water
Wishy-washed, the blind thing, and the corally seapinks
Nodded over my hand. How can there be a revelation
In a world so full it couldn't be more full?

The pigeon hurtled out of my life. And I don't remember
The eagle going away. But I'll never forget
The eagle-shaped space it left, stamped on the air.
Absence or presence? . . . It seems I'm on a ledge of seapinks
All the time, an observing, blank-puzzled cliff-hanger.

February 1973

Reversal

She showed me a polished pebble with a salmon fly
Painted on it. Local arts and crafts
Scrabble on beaches for an addled egg left
By a mountain, varnish it, make it domestic
And tart it up with a minuscule landscape,
An improbable flower or a salmon fly.

How tunes diminish when they become domestic.
Grace notes fall off, the lamentable, sour
Flat note climbs up that ruinous semitone
And there's the tune's ghost – a flabby ghost,
All its bonestructure gone. It tamely
Toddles the house, slippered, domestic.

Once in a peatbog I found – no ghost –
A blue hare's skeleton. It was its self,
Running dead still . . . Girl with the pebble,
I'll put you out in a wildness that'll tune
Bones and bones to glimmer back in you,
My homely nobody, my skin and ghost.

And seas will break on the pebble, the tune
Be restored to a state of gracenotes – for
Wildness is not wilderness. By the fire
I'll watch your true self moving dead still.
And you and I will, in that artful wildness,
Come into harmony out of tune.

May 1973

[99]

Stag in a neglected hayfield

He's not in his blazing red yet. His antlers
Are a foot that'll be a spreading yard.
The field was a hayfield: now a heifer
And two cows graze there and no dog barks.

That's the outward scene. The inner –
A mountain forgotten, a remembered man.
The deer will return to the hill: but stiller
Than the stone above them are the scything hands.

June 1973

A. K.'s summer hut

It clamps itself to a rock, like a limpet,
And creeps up and down in a tide of people,
Hardly ever stranded in a tideless sabbath:
A pilgrimage place where all hymns are jubilant.

The starry revolutions around it,
The deer circling in new foundations
Of old worlds, the immortal noise
Of the river ghosted with salmon – these

Are a bloodstream it's a blood-drop in.
Such sharing. Such giving. See, at the window,
That silly chaffinch, practically talking Gaelic,
And the eiders domestic as farmyard ducks

And the lady gull yacking for her breakfast.
If I were a bethlehemish star I'd stand fixed
Over that roof, knowing there'd be born there
No wars, no tortures, no savage crucifixions.

But a rare, an extraordinary thing –
An exhilaration of peace, a sounding
Grace with trinities galore – if only
Those three collared doves in the rowan tree.

July 1973

Small rain

The rain – it was a little rain – walked through the wood
   (a little wood)
Leaving behind unexpected decorations and delicacies
On the fox by the dyke, that was eating a salmon's head.
(The poacher who had hidden it wasn't going to be pleased.)

The rain whisperingly went on, past the cliff all Picasso'd
With profiles, blackening the Stoer peat stacks, silvering
Forty sheep's backs, half smudging out a buzzard.
It reached us. It passed us, totally unimpressed.

Not me. I looked at you, all cobwebby with seeds of water,
Changed from Summer to Spring. I had absolutely no way of saying
How vivid can be unemphatic, how bright can be brighter
Than brightness. You knew, though. You were smiling, and no
   wonder.

December 1973

Praise of a road

You won't let me forget you. You keep nudging me
With your hairpin bends or, without a *Next, please*,
Magic-lanterning another prodigious view
In my skull where I sit in the dark with my brains.

You turn up your nose above Loch Hope,
That effete low-lier where men sit comfy
In boats, casting for seatrout, and whisper
Up the hill, round the crag – there are the Crocachs.

You're an acrobat with a bulrushy spine,
Looping in air, turning to look at yourself
And faultlessly skidding on your own stones
Round improbable corners and arriving safe.

When the Crocachs have given me mist and trout
And clogs of peat, how I greet you and whirl
Down your half-scree zigzags, tumbling like a peewit
Through trembling evenings down to Loch Eriboll.

                    January 1974

Praise of a collie

She was a small dog, neat and fluid –
Even her conversation was tiny:
She greeted you with *bow*, never *bow-wow*.

Her sons stood monumentally over her
But did what she told them. Each grew grizzled
Till it seemed he was his own mother's grandfather.

Once, gathering sheep on a showery day,
I remarked how dry she was. Pollóchan said, 'Ah,
It would take a very accurate drop to hit Lassie.'

She sailed in the dinghy like a proper sea-dog.
Where's a burn? – she's first on the other side.
She flowed through fences like a piece of black wind.

But suddenly she was old and sick and crippled . . .
I grieved for Pollóchan when he took her a stroll
And put his gun to the back of her head.

January 1974

Praise of a boat

The *Bateau Ivre* and the *Marie Celeste*,
The *Flying Dutchman* hurdling latitudes –
You could make a list (sad ones like the *Lusitania*
And brave puffed-up ones like the *Mayflower*).

Mine's called *the boat*. It's a quiet, anonymous one
That needs my two arms to drag it through the water.
It takes me huge distances of a few miles
From its lair in Loch Roe to fishy Soya.

It prances on the spot in its watery stable.
It butts the running tide with a bull's head.
It skims downwind, planing like a shearwater.
In crossrips it's awkward as a piano.

And what a coffin it is for haddocks
And bomb-shaped lythe and tigerish mackerel –
Though it once met a basking shark with a bump
And sailed for a while looking over its shoulder.

When salmon are about it goes glib in the dark,
Whispering a net out over the sternsheets –
How it crabs the tide-rush, the cunning thing,
While arms plunge down for the wrestling silver.

Boat of no dreams, you open spaces
The mind can't think of till it's in them,
Where the world is easy and dangerous and
Who can distinguish saints and sinners?

Sometimes that space reaches out
Till I'm enclosed in it in stony Edinburgh
And I hear you like a barrel thumping on head waves
Or in still water gurgling like a baby.

January 1974

Praise of a thorn bush

You've taken your stand
between Christy MacLeod's house
and the farthest planet.

The ideal shape of a circle
means nothing to you: you're all
armpits and elbows
and scraggy fingers that hold so delicately
a few lucid roses. You are
an encyclopedia of angles.

At night you trap stars, and the moon
fills you with distances.
I arrange myself to put
one rose in the belt of Orion.

When the salt gales drag through you
you whip them with flowers
and I think –
Exclamations for you, little rose bush,
and a couple of fanfares.

                                    January 1974

Small lochs

He's obsessed with clocks, she with politics,
He with motor cars, she with amber and jet.
There's something to be obsessed with for all of us.
Mine is lochs, the smaller the better.

I look at the big ones – Loch Ness, Loch Lomond,
Loch Shin, Loch Tay – and I bow respectfully,
But they're too grand to be invited home.
How could I treat them in the way they'd expect?

But the Dog Loch runs in eights when I go walking.
The Cat Loch purrs on the windowsill. I wade
Along Princes Street through Loch na Barrack.
In smoky bars I tell them like beads.

And don't think it's just the big ones that are lordlily named.
I met one once and when I asked what she was called
The little thing said (without blushing, mind you)
The Loch of the Corrie of the Green Waterfalls.

I know they're just H_2O in a hollow.
Yet not much time passes without me thinking of them
Dandling lilies and talking sleepily
And standing huge mountains on their watery heads.

December 1974

Stonechat on Cul Beg

A flint-on-flint ticking – and there he is,
Trim and dandy – in square miles of bracken
And bogs and boulders a tiny work of art,
Bright as an illumination on a monkish parchment.

I queue up to watch him. He makes me a group
Of solemn connoisseurs trying to see the brushstrokes.
I want to thumb the air in their knowing way.
I murmur *Chinese black*, I murmur *alizarin*.

But the little picture with four flirts and a delicate
Up-swinging's landed on another boulder.
He gives me a stained-glass look and keeps
Chick-chacking at me. I suppose he's swearing.

You'd expect something like oboes or piccolos
(Though other birds, too, have pebbles in their throats –
And of them I love best the airy skylark
Twittering like marbles squeezed in your fist).

Cul Beg looks away – his show's been stolen.
And the up-staged loch would yawn if it could.
Only the benign sun in his fatherly way
Beams on his bright child throwing a tantrum.

March 1975

Summer evening in Assynt

The green of Elphin
in this particular light
is its particular green.
It might be worn
by a royal, pale girl
in a Celtic legend.

I look up
at the eagle idling over
from Kylesku.
I look away
at the shattering waterblink
of Loch Cama.

I look down at my feet
and there's a frog
so green, so beautiful
it might be waiting in a Celtic legend
for the kind girl to come
with her gentle kiss:
for the spell to go backward.

August 1975

1,800 feet up

The flower – it didn't know it –
was called dwarf cornel.
I found this out by enquiring.

Now I remember the name
but have forgotten the flower.

– The curse of literacy.

And the greed for knowing. –
I'll have to contour again
from the Loch of the Red Corrie
to the Loch of the Green Corrie
to find what doesn't know its name,
to find what doesn't even know
it's a flower.

Since I believe in correspondences
I shrink in my many weathers
from whoever is contouring immeasurable space
to find what I am like – this forgotten thing
he once gave a name to.

November 1975

The following twelve poems are presented in sequence, as in their original publication.

Notes on a winter journey, and a footnote

1

The snow's almost faultless. It bounces back
the sun's light but can do nothing with
those two stags, their cold noses, their yellow teeth.

2

On the loch's eye a cataract is forming.
Fistfuls of white make the telephone wires
loop after loop of snow buntings.

3

So few cars, they leave the snow snow.
I think of the horrible marzipan
in the streets of Edinburgh.

4

The hotel at Ullapool, that should be a bang of light,
is crepuscular. The bar is fireflied
with whisky glasses.

5

At Inchnadamph snow is falling. The windscreen wipers
squeak and I stare through
a segment of a circle. What more do I ever do? . . .

6

(Seventeen miles to go. I didn't know it, but when
I got there a death waited for me – that segment
shut its fan: and a blinding winter closed in.)

April 1976

A. K. MacLeod

I went to the landscape I love best
and the man who was its meaning and added to it
met me at Ullapool.

The beautiful landscape was under snow
and was beautiful in a new way.

Next morning, the man who had greeted me
with the pleasure of pleasure
vomited blood
and died.

Crofters and fishermen and womenfolk, unable
to say any more, said,
'It's a grand day, it's a beautiful day.'

And I thought, 'Yes, it is.'
And I thought of him lying there,
the dead centre of it all.

March 1976

Highland funeral

Over the dead man's house, over his landscape
the frozen air was a scrawny psalm
I believed in, because it was pagan
as he was.

Into it the minister's voice
spread a pollution of bad beliefs.
The sanctimonious voice dwindled away
over the boring, beautiful sea.

The sea was boring, as grief is,
but beautiful, as grief is not.
Through grief's dark ugliness I saw that beauty
because he would have.

And that darkened the ugliness . . . Can the dead
help? I say so. Because, a year later,
that sanctimonious voice is silent and the pagan
landscape is sacred in a new way.

January 1977

A month after his death

An accordion and a fiddle
fit nimbly together their different natures
with such bouncing wit it makes small
the darkness outside that goes straight up
for ever and ever.

Out there are the dregs of history. Out there
mindlessness lashes the sea against the sea-wall:
and a bird flies screaming over the roof.

We laugh and we sing, but we all know we're thinking
of the one who isn't here.

The laughter and the singing are paper flowers
laid on a wet grave in an empty darkness.
For we all know we're thinking
of the one who can't be here,
not even as a ghost smiling through the black window.

January 1978

Triple burden

I know I had my death in me
from the moment I yelled upside-down
in the world.

Now I have another death in me: yours.
Each is the image of the other.

To carry two deaths
is a burden for any man:
and it's a heavy knowledge that tells me
only the death I was born with
will destroy the other.

For a boat has sailed into
the sea of unknowing;
you are on board.

And somewhere another boat
rocks
by another pier.

It's waiting to take me
where I'll never know you again –
a voyage
beyond knowledge, beyond memory.

May 1977

Comforter

Thank God you don't tell
me to stop thinking of him –
that I'm grieving, not for him,
but for my loss
– for, though that's true,
my grief is also
his celebration of me.

February 1977

Praise of a man

He went through a company like a lamplighter –
see the dull minds, one after another,
begin to glow, to shed
a benificent light.

He went through a company like
a knifegrinder – see the dull minds
scattering sparks of themselves,
becoming razory, becoming useful.

He went through a company
as himself. But now he's one
of the multitudinous company of the dead
where are no individuals.

The benificent lights dim
but don't vanish. The razory edges
dull but still cut. He's gone: but you can see
his tracks still, in the snow of the world.

November 1977

From his house door

I say to myself, How he enriched my life.
And I say to myself, More than he have died,
he's not the only one.

I look at the estuary and see
a gravel bank and a glitter going through it
and the stealthy tide, black-masked,
drowning stone after stone.

June 1977

Angus's dog

Black collie, do you remember yourself?

Do you remember your name was Mephistopheles,
though (as if you were only a little devil)
everyone called you Meph?

You'd chase everything – sea gulls, motor cars,
jet planes. (It's said you once set off
after a lightning flash.) Half over a rock,
you followed the salmon fly arcing
through the bronze water. You loved everything
except rabbits – though
you grinned away under the bed
when your master came home
drink taken. How you'd lay your head
on a visitor's knee and look up, so soulfully,
like George Eliot playing Sarah Bernhardt.

... Black Meph, how can you remember yourself
in that blank no-time, no-place where
you can't even greet your master
though he's there too?

December 1977

Dead friend

How do I meet
a man who's no longer there?
How can I lament the loss
of a man who won't go away?
How can I be changed
by changelessness?

I stand in my gloomy field
like a Pictish carving
that keeps its meaning but is, too, weathered
into another one.

February 1977

In memoriam

On that stormy night
a top branch broke off
on the biggest tree in my garden.

It's still up there. Though its leaves
are withered black among the green
the living branches
won't let it fall.

November 1976

Defeat

What I think of him,
what I remember of him
are gifts I can't give
to anyone.

For all I can say of him
is no more
than a scribble in the margin
of a lost manuscript.

January 1978

End of Poems for Angus sequence

Tighnuilt – the House of the Small Stream

for Charlie Ross

In a corner of Kirkaig,
in a wild landscape, he created
a garden, a small Eden
of fruit trees, flowers and regimental
vegetables. Such labour. Such love.

It's still there, though he is not.
To remember him is to put that garden
in another place. It shines
in the desolate landscape of loss –
a small Eden, of use and of beauty.

I visit him there
between the mountains and the sea.
We sit by a small stream
that will never run dry.

February 1977

Off Coigeach Point

Flat sea, thin mist
and a seal singing.
– And the world's an old man in his corner
telling a folktale.

Haddock goggle up, are
swung aboard. Gray as the sea mist.
They drown in air.

In the fishbox they
have nothing to do with death. They've become
a fine-line drawing
in the art gallery
of the world.

We make for home.

Near Soya
Seven seals oilily slide off a skerry
into the silky gray. Norman tells me
if he puts the engine into reverse
they turn
a back somersault.

And he does.
And they do.

June 1977

Me as traveller

The toy yacht and the clockwork liner
were bad prophets. I was to be
a bold rover? I was to carry the globe
in a stringbag of voyages?

Happy the man, I mutter,
who's had no need to travel
anywhere. I crisscross the glebe
of small Scotland and settle for
one small part of it.

America, Italy, Canada, I rested on you
briefly as a butterfly and returned
to suck the honey of Assynt
and want no more, though that honey
has three bitternesses in it, three deaths
more foreign to me
than the other side of space.

September 1977

'NOTATIONS'

Notations of ten summer minutes

A boy skips flat stones out to sea – each does fine
till a small wave meets it head on and swallows it.
The boy will do the same.

The schoolmaster stands looking out of the window
with one Latin eye and one Greek one.
A boat rounds the point in Gaelic.

Out of the shop comes a stream
of Omo, Weetabix, BiSoDol tablets and a man
with a pocket shaped like a whisky bottle.

Lord V. walks by with the village in his pocket.
Angus walks by
spending the village into the air.

A melodeon is wheezing a clear-throated jig
on the deck of the *Arcadia*. On the shore hills Pan
cocks a hairy ear; and falls asleep again.

The ten minutes are up, except they aren't.
I leave the village, except I don't.
The jig fades to silence, except it doesn't.

April 1976

Highland games

They sit on the heather slopes
and stand six deep round the rope ring.
Keepers and shepherds in their best plus-fours
who live mountains apart
exchange gossip and tall stories.
Women hand out sandwiches,
rock prams and exchange
small stories and gossip.
The Chieftain leans his English accent
on a five-foot crook and feels
one of the natives.

The rope ring is full
of strenuous metaphors.
Eight runners shoulder each other
eight times round it – a mile
against the clock that will kill them.

Little girls breasted only with medals translate
a tune that will outlast them
with formalised legs and
antler arms. High jumpers
come down to earth and,
in the centre
a waddling 'heavy' tries to throw
the tree of life in one straight line.

Thank God for the bar, thank God
for the Games Night Dance – even though they end
in the long walk home
with people no longer here – with exiles and deaths –
your nearest companions.

May 1977

View with no prospect

Though I'm in sunlight
a dangling shower drifts across the hill called
Durlain and across the eagle's nest on it.
Below, the Loch of the Thicket of the Fawns
tickles with the slight drops. Once, here, in one forenoon
I met and killed four adders. Fool.

My head's full of landscapes and their creatures.
My head's full of a handful of people, a few alive
as the lizard basking on that stone, a few
dead as the stone.

I wish I could wish those adders alive again.

But: thank God I don't get tired of ghosts.
Their tobacco smoke slowly writhes up and away.
Voices laugh. Heads nod wisely. And a collie stares
at nothing at all, and sees it, teaching me to do the same.

April 1980

Toad

Stop looking like a purse. How could a purse
squeeze under the rickety door and sit,
full of satisfaction, in a man's house?

You clamber towards me on your four corners –
right hand, left foot, left hand, right foot.

I love you for being a toad,
for crawling like a Japanese wrestler,
and for not being frightened.

I put you in my purse hand, not shutting it,
and set you down outside directly under
every star.

A jewel in your head? Toad,
you've put one in mine,
a tiny radiance in a dark place.

December 1978

Local dance

In a corner of the village hall
five children sit behind their big round eyes.

Below the trashy decorations their elders dance,
thumping and Bruegelish. In the band
Ian Shimag, staring into another world,
spiders his fingers up and down
his Lazarus accordeon. And the night outside
goes away.

Wee Mary in the corner gets up and starts
dancing alone. The night inside her
goes away and she performs
dulcet rituals in a language of arms and legs
in the world Ian Shimag was staring at. And the stamping fishermen

and their bouncing ladies, capering by,
look at her with affection, remembering
when the night inside them used to go away
so long ago.

September 1980

Gamekeeper's widow

She opens the door as if she has a right to.
She sits among the furniture as though
she were alien to it, or it to her.

Except, his gun on the wall, his crooks, his telescope
speak to her from an immeasurable distance
and she hears every word they say.

Outside, the garden he had created
is slowly dying back
to the wilderness it came from.

Like me, she thinks: and rises and goes
into the kitchen, glancing at the useless telescope,
lightly touching the brutal gun.

October 1980

Invasion of bees

Between the ceiling and the roof
whole fields were humming.

Or, add to one bee a thousand others and it becomes
a dynamo.

A man was fetched from Helmsdale.
He carried a vicious brass pump.

It switched off that dynamo, it reaped
whole fields and heather slopes.

And a summer inside a summer
died, leaving a useless crop.

I have a summer inside my summer.
I cherish it. It's flowery and heathery.

Terrified, I dream of a man from Helmsdale
walking towards me, a sack in his hand.

December 1980

Two thieves

At the Place for Pulling up Boats
(one word in Gaelic) the tide is full.
It seeps over the grass, stealthy as a robber.
Which it is.

– For old Flora tells me
that fifty yards stretch of gravel, now under water,
was, in her granny's time, a smooth green sward
where the Duke of Sutherland
turned his coach and four.

What an image of richness, a tiny pageantry
in this small dying place
whose every house is now lived in
by the sad widow of a fine strong man.

There were fine strong men in the Duke's time.
He drove them to the shore, he drove them
to Canada. He gave no friendly thought to them
as he turned his coach and four
on the sweet green sward
by the Place for Pulling up Boats
where no boats are.

December 1980

Camera man

Six rods are dapping for sea trout
On Loch Baddagyle. Their blowlines each make
A bosomy downwind curve. Six bushy flies
Ballet dance on the sunstruck water.

– See that boulder? In its toupee of heather
There's a wild cat watching me. Two topazes with ears.
. . . I tilt up and pan along my trail of mountains
From Ben More Coigach all the way to Quinag.

An old ewe brings me down to the earth
She stamps her forefoot on. I look at her implacable
Whisky and soda eyes. She knows all a sheep
Needs to know: she's a black-stockinged bluestocking.

And a spinnaker line has straightened. The water
Explodes and shoots a sea trout into the air,
While five bushy flies still dance on the moving glitter,
Little water nymphs in their dangerous tutus.

February 1981

One more

That's it, said the stag
and buckled his front legs and fell over.

The stalker went up on a jet of exaltation
and sank down again.

That's it, he thought, watching
a hind leg give its last kick.

And premonitions bumped like gun shots
among the corries.

But nothing cared, nothing cared at all,
except the man and the stag.

The small burn gabbled by and in the Red Corrie
another stag mounted a hind among the small flowers.

And the minutes filed by, all anonymous,
each with a gralloching knife in its belt.

April 1981

Summer idyll

Under a ferocious snowfall
of gulls and fulmars
a corner of the bay is simmering
with herring fry.

Into them slice
Assyrian hosts
of mackerel.

Sweet day, so cool, so calm, so bright . . .

Three porpoises pronounce
three puffs and cavalry charge
into the Assyrians.

Clouds lisp across the sky in a trance of silence.

Farther out, a commando of killer whales
grin and leap.
They're setting their ambush
for the cavalry.

And in the gentle West
a ladylike sunset
swoons
on the chaise-longue
of the Hebrides.

June 1981

Running bull

All his weight's forward.
He looks like a big black hunchback
with a small black boy running behind him.

Put an invisible sixpence on the ground –
he'll turn on it.
So don't, if he's facing away from you.
People scatter. I scatter too.

Sometimes he stops
and looks redly around, wondering
which new direction
to hurtle at.

Donald saunters towards him.
The bull glowers at him
from between his knees.

And his fire goes out! . . . He puts on a nonchalance
and swaggers towards the byre, followed
by sauntering Orpheus.

July 1981

On the Lairg to Lochinver bus

I travel West, a smudged figure
among people in four rows
divided in two.

The driver chain smokes. I know him.
Inside his bald head are microfilms
of poaching stags, loose women
and half bottles at Brackloch.

A young tourist (Scandinavian?)
stares at a map while the true facts
slide by the window.

We're apt to do that.

I've a map of tomorrow.
When I get there
I'll look round anxiously to see
if it's out of date.

If the broken gate is mended,
if old Flora is still alive,
if the tide still comes in
and goes out.

November 1981

Pastoral

The road folds itself half round a tree
and sets off at a new angle, seeming
pleased with the change.

It's not much of a road. It's been made
more by carts than men.

It bumps its nose against Lachie's house
and stops there
in the blue scent a peat fire makes,
in the cosy noises the brown hens make.

The cock, in the amazing uniform
of a wildly foreign Field Marshal,
scans two worlds through his monoculars.

– No enemy in sight . . . The Field Marshal becomes
a Pioneer Corps private in drag
and half-heartedly scratches the scratches
on the homely ground.

November 1981

Found guilty

To this day, poor swimmer as I am,
it grieves me
that I watched the little sandpiper drown.

When I passed the nest
shoulder high on a bank of Loch Lurgain
the young ones cheeped-cheeped out of it
to flop in the heather twenty yards away.

Except that one. It flew over the water,
lower and lower, then tried to fly in the water:
and drowned.

I've watched friends, strong fliers among mountains,
who flew lower and lower
and drowned in the uncaring water
they had soared above.

Little sandpiper, you left me
accused of what
I have no defence against.

Friends, I ask your forgiveness.
I ask for something
I don't deserve. And I ask for it
too late.

December 1981

Highland barbecue

Darkness has come,
snuffing the candles of distance,
binding the legs of the tall ash trees
with black bandages.

By the Red Rock Pool
the youngsters of the village
have their barbecue going and near it
a bonfire of logs
and broken fishboxes. The flames jig
to the jigging of Jimac's accordion.

From a distance it looks like
a tiny, mediaeval hell – all that red,
those figures in the flicker.

But come close. It's a heavenly glebe
of charred sausages and laughter,
of young seraphs licking their fingers
and adding to the jewel heap
of praise-the-Lord
Coca-Cola tins.

They pay no heed, in their short-lived holiness,
to the gull over the bay
– rejected spirit
lamenting in the desolation
of the outer darkness.

May 1984

On the north side of Suilven

The three-inch-wide streamlet
trickles over its own fingers
down the sandstone slabs
of my favourite mountain.

Like the Amazon it'll reach the sea.
Like the Volga
it'll forget its own language there.

Its water goes down my throat
with a glassy coldness,
like something suddenly remembered.

I drink
its freezing vocabulary
and half understand the purity
of all beginnings.

May 1984

At the Loch of the Pass of the Swans

I dangle my feet in the cool loch water.
A thousand journeys, a century of miles
crinkle to the crimson flower beside me.

Where is the mist that wrapped itself round
the threshing machine last autumn?
Where's the blackface lamb I pulled from a peat bog?

Where are the places my father knew
and the storm waves roaring in the caves of Scarp,
frightening my little girl mother?

Escape from my history – to the campfires
of Huns and Goths, to the monks picking
hazel nuts and berries on sunny Iona.

I play with time and distance,
a game less cruel than the one
they play with me, the one they will win.

Let them. For this moment they've shrunk
to the crimson flower beside me
and two feet, corpse-white, in the smiling water.

May 1984

Everywhere at Loch Roe

The brown dinghy labours round the point
like a damaged insect – only two legs left.

I stand on a rock
that's shrugged in a gray coat of barnacles.
The sea keeps slapping it.

The slaps measure time, I think, idly.

– Not me.
I've given up time for the moment.
I'll have nothing to do with it.

The tall girl backs the dinghy in
and I step aboard.

I take the oars and pull
against the wind and tide.
In out, in out. Measuring time
the hard way.

My turn to round the first point,
caught again in the old rhythm –
time and headland, time and headland
and a quiet bay at the end of it.

July 1984

A man walking through Clachtoll

He carries a scythe, but he's young,
he doesn't notice symbols.

Packs of waves hold the Split Rock at bay.
He pays no need to their growling and slavering.

He's thinking of Mairi at the dance tonight.
She's his Aurora, she's his Merry Dancer.

They'll whirl in and out of six other lives and end
teetotuming alone. By God, they'll *Strip the Willow*.

He turns into the field and sets to work.
He rejects symbols. But he is one all the same.

And the hay falls and the dances end.
And the scythe cuts, no matter who's holding it.

August 1984

On the pier at Kinlochbervie

The stars go out one by one
as though a bluetit the size of the world
were pecking them like peanuts out of the sky's string bag,

A ludicrous image, I know.

Take away the gray light.
I want the bronze shields of summer
or winter's scalding sleet.

My mind is struggling with itself.

That fishing boat is a secret
approaching me. It's a secret
coming out of another one.
I want to know the first one of all.

Everything's in the distance,
as I am. I wish I could flip that distance
like a cigarette into the water.

I want an extreme of nearness.
I want boundaries on my mind.
I want to feel the world like a straitjacket.

September 1984

Haymaking

What will the corncrake do now?
Where will the bad hen, the black one, lay her eggs?

Through sunny days we scythed
the trembling grass. We turned it.
We heaped it in small hills.

We trundled barrowloads
to the shed and piled it
high to the roof.

Today, we've pressed it down
in a scent of dust and honey
and piled it high to the roof again.

I lean, sweating, on the hay rake
in the hay coloured sun. My neck
is tickly. My eyes itch.

I am full of joy – and I add to it
with a vast, unmelodious sneeze.

December 1984

'HONEY AND SALT'

Between mountain and sea

Honey and salt – land smell and sea smell,
as in the long ago, as in forever.

The days pick me up and carry me off,
half-child, half-prisoner,

on their journey that I'll share
for a while.

They wound and they bless me
with strange gifts:

the salt of absence,
the honey of memory.

December 1984

On a croft by the Kirkaig

The cock, king of the croft, crowed,
tearing a jagged rip in the silence
that even the river washing by
had failed to disturb.

My mind was like the silence:
an equivalence of peace.

But the cock crowed, ushering in
another day at midday.
What day?

And into my mind came the man
with whom, so often, I'd sat by that river,
now in the most rounded silence of all
where no river shuffles by
and no cock will ever crow again.

I'm sad
but not sad only,
for I share his possessions
and therefore himself.

Cherishingly, I count three of them –
the equivalence of peace,
the cock, carved on tiptoe
on the gold coin of himself,

and the river bundling its sweet vocabulary
towards the swarming languages
of the sea.

January 1985

Crofter

Last thing at night
he steps outside to breathe
the smell of winter.

The stars, so shy in summer,
glare down
from a huge emptiness.

In a huge silence he listens
for small sounds. His eyes
are filled with friendliness.

What's history to him?
He's an emblem of it
in its pure state.

And proves it. He goes inside.
The door closes and the light
dies in the window.

January 1985

On Lachie's croft

On Lachie's croft the cock stands
under the wheelbarrow. What's wrong? – He's bedraggled.
Where are his military elegance,
his gauleiter manners, his insufferable conceit?
I'll call him rooster, it seems more fitting.

I, too, feel bedraggled and haphazard; something
has filched my compass, I'm breathing black air.
I look at that rooster, I look at me.
His hens scratch the ground, step back
and peer at the scratches. They make
motherly sounds, so cosy, so fireside.

But he opens his gummy eyes, looks at me
and utters, no tortured trumpet call,
but a barren croak.

I breathe black air, I poke at
my rumpled feathers, I can't stand on tiptoe.
How I miss my cosy brown hens.
How I miss their motherly clucking.
I'm master of nothing I survey.

October 1986

Perfect evening, Loch Roe

I pull the boat along gently. In the stern
Donald tucks his long rod under his arm
and lights his pipe.

Behind my right shoulder
the cliff Salpioder holds out
its anvil nose
over the sea.

The distances of other times,
the unmeasurable ones,
have withdrawn into nowhere at all.

– A sudden clamour. Oystercatchers
fly off from a gray rock –
their orange-red beaks; their wingbars flashing white.

The desires of other times too
have disappeared
behind the desires that lay beyond them.

And the dreams of other times
are huddled in their false country,
exiles returned to their homeland.

I feel something like love.
I can spare it, for the source of it all
is waiting, there, in the squat cottage.

November 1986

Wester Ross, West Sutherland

The mountains swirl water
from their high lochs. It comes down
in fraying threads.

A country of old wars, of clan battles
led by men we call heroes.
The mountains will see them no more.
Yet people remain whose courage is
to live in this hard landscape –
and refuse to leave it.

The sources they came from
have not dried up.

Such few people. Such thin threads
still spilling down
from the high lochs that never dry.

June 1987

Sargasso Sea

Tangled in weeds.
Far from home.
On an ocean
I've nothing to do with.

How I envy the elvers
who leave their Sargasso and drift
across the Atlantic.

So many will find
the river I know best.
How eagerly they swim
against its rushing torrent

that brings them news
from high places
I once visited
long ago.

November 1988

Maps

Planning a journey
is always a bit frightening –
all those contour lines on the hills:
that blue wriggle meaning a stream:
a small dot that turns out to be a city.

If only one could swallow the map –
including the creatures that aren't in it
and the absence of tomorrow
and the presence of rain showers –
and all the time sit,
a geographer of distinction,
in one's usual chair
lighting another cigarette
and planning such meals,
such expeditions.

December 1988

The Loch of the Peevish Creek

A name like that – how can I not
write about you?

I fished you only once
in your handsome surroundings
and learned why you have that name,
for all I caught were half a dozen trout
and small ones at that.

And how often, in my metaphorical mood,
have I cast flies in other places,
say, over the metaphorical waters of poetry,
knowing the lordly trout that are in them
and catching fingerling after fingerling.

But just because sometimes they relent
and send me stumbling home
with a broad tail

sticking out of my fishing bag
I come back again and again
to their peevish waters, wondering –
my fishing bag, this time, will it be light or heavy?

February 1989

Idling at sea

I let the boat drift and look around
at the mountains I know best
with their beautiful Gaelic names.

As though I'm sitting on a tiny private star
drifting at a thousand miles a minute
through an uncountable galaxy.

As though a thought revealed
a thousand thoughts that I can observe
but never inhabit.

As though our homely earth
whispers to me *Cousin*. As though
happiness can shelter even in a drifting boat.

February 1989

At the foot of Cul Mor

A mountain half a mile away,
and a stonechat twenty yards.
Boulders and deergrass. And a loch
juggling with the weightless sunshine.
I stand among them. They let me
– except the stonechat. He doesn't want me here.
That's his only idea.
The other things have none. And no more have I.
Yet I'm translating
their language which has no dictionary
into feelings that have no words.
I bless them in my pagan way.
They pay no heed, in theirs.
But, without knowing it, they bless me too,
even the stonechat
with his bravado, with his spiky insults
and his dancing flight from boulder to boulder.

March 1989

Two men at once

In the Culag Bar a fiddler is playing
fast-rippling tunes with easy dexterity.

How do I know? I'm in Edinburgh.

On the pier, sun-scorched tourists
hang their bellies over improbable shorts.

How do I know? I'm in Edinburgh.

In the Veyatie burn a man
hooks a trout. It starts rampaging.

And I'm in Edinburgh.

Or so I say. How easy to be
two men at once.

One smiling and drinking coffee
in Leamington Terrace, Edinburgh.

The other cutting the pack of memories
and turning up ace after ace after ace.

April 1989

Country lover

Back from walking among mountains
where he was alone but not lonely,
he sits by the fire
feeling like three men round a table, all of them drinking and talking.

Each counters a memory
with another one, he tries to listen
to them all.

– Three histories of a day
land in a muddle on the table,
and no waiter in the world
to wipe them away.

Alone but not lonely
he smiles at the fire, in a room
filled with mountains and lochs
and flowery boglands.

September 1989

Sunset at Clashnessie

Two long thin clouds
are cutting the sun in slices.
It's helpless. It's dying in hospital.
And there are no stars yet
to bring it a bunch of constellations
and a coloured box of planets.

Yesterday seems far away.
We've crossed another border
into today, whose language
we're just beginning to learn.

The two clouds thicken
and I stare at the sun
crumbling away
into the darkness that'll finish it off.

How few of today's words
we'll remember tomorrow
when the Lazarus sun
steps out into the glory he died in.

October 1989

Things behind each other

In between the notes of the music
porpoises curve up and over
in the sea I keep thinking of.

That long, savage phrase –
dragonflies by the Fiag burn
are snapping up horseflies.

Pianissimo it goes
and so many daybreaks
quietly spread out from horizons.

Now the slow movement –
sad as the men walking from Kirkaig
to the graveyard at Lochinver.
And the finale – a burst of joy.
And I settle down with the world,
counting nothing, being one of the total.

January 1991

In the croft house called The Glen

Where now are the gloomy thoughts? . . .

Outside the new lambs
are nuzzling their mothers
and a freezing wind is saying
 Stay indoors.
I will. And peace, that old
fashioned thing,
settles herself on the sofa
and looks at me with forgotten eyes.

I love her gray hairs
and her hands clasped in her lap
as though holding a precious thing –
and talking with a quiet voice
that drowns the noisy world
with its gloomy thoughts
and hectoring demands.

It's night now.
I've no fear of going to sleep
I've no fear of waking in the morning.
For peace will say, Today
is like yesterday
and I'll be here for the long
length of it.

April 1991

Image of a man

Into a tiny bay at Loch Roe, a tall yacht
groped, and anchored.
So many years ago. Why do I remember it?
Is it because of the tinyness of the bay?
Is it because of the size of the yacht
and its sails fumbling down and furled?
Or is it because it was like a man I knew
who lived in the tiny village nearby?
A man splendid as that yacht, with a crew
of thoughts that were sad and merry
until the strange sails that carried him
fumbled down and were furled for the last time.

May 1991

Assynt and Edinburgh

From the corner of Scotland I know so well
I see Edinburgh sprawling like seven cats
on its seven hills beside the Firth of Forth.

And when I'm in Edinburgh I walk
amongst the mountains and lochs of that corner
that looks across the Minch to the Hebrides.

Two places I belong to as though I was born
in both of them.

They make every day a birthday,
giving me gifts wrapped in the ribbons of memory.
I store them away, greedy as a miser.

September 1991

Gale at Stoer Point

The wind roars through the hot sunlight.
Great waves tower up and smash their foreheads
On the sandstone cliff, savagely exhilarated
As though they thought that this time, at last,
They'd bring down the lighthouse to be chewed at leisure.

They don't think, of course. They're pushed by the wind
And hauled by the moon ... Just like me, I thought,
Smashing my forehead against other cliffs.
Forget that. Let me savour the satiny brows
Punched into brain froth by the stolid sandstone.

And the fulmars, feather boats with tubes for nostrils,
Glide and soar on the windy turbulence
With such careless skill I feel like a moorhen,
That red-faced skulker by tame ponds ... Have I, too,
Longtoed green legs with neat red garters?

Date not known

A small corner with a space in it

Into the Heather Pool
the river tumbles
over boulders:
a row of white fists.

They open out
into one flat palm
that splays into fingers of water
pointing towards the sea.

A trio of sounds!
angry roar,
gentle plainsong,
childish chattering.

And no summer or winter,
just weather,
quick-change artist
that never leaves the stage.

                              Date not known

On Handa

The cliffs are so high I look down
on the backs of seabirds
perched on the narrowest of ledges
or wheeling and diving or
scuttering on the surface,
and all as different as the tribes
of men
from comical puffins to
rapscallion skuas
bullying the gulls to drop
the fish they've just caught.

Date not known

Processes

The river slides by, looking harmless.
Ask the rock, that gets smaller and smaller
from its stroking.

Birch trees swarm up the opposite bank
in groups that die, so slowly,
from the centre outwards.
The stalker's path up there
is being taken back into the hill.
Quagmires have swallowed what were stones.

These three things are happening to me also.
Yet I happily observe them from the peace
they bring to me, even in their dying.

I'm a crofter in the landscape of time
repairing a tumbling wall
with each dead stone balanced on another.

                                        January 1992

By the Three Lochans

I sit, trying to look like a heather bush –
hoping to see
a mewing buzzard or a vole or a dragonfly.
How quickly the days slide away
into where they came from.

It's hard to change anything.
I look into my hand to see
if there's an idea there
giving birth to a strenuous baby.
Only a life-line that's not long enough.

An obstinate old rowan tree
stands on a tiny island.
So many storms, yet there it is
with only a few berries, each determined
to be the last one to drop into the water.

And the light floods down
revealing mountains and flowers
and so many shadows. If only
a merlin would hurtle past, that atom
of speed, that molecule of life.

January 1992

INDEX OF TITLES